THE WOLF AT THE DOOR

MARK SILVERTHORN

THE WOLF
AT THE DOOR

WHAT TO DO WHEN
COLLECTION AGENCIES
COME CALLING

McClelland & Stewart

Library and Archives Canada Cataloguing in Publication

Silverthorn, Mark Anthony
    The wolf at the door : what to do when collection agencies come calling / Mark Anthony Silverthorn.

ISBN 978-0-7710-8036-4

1. Collecting of accounts – Canada. 2. Collection agencies – Canada.
3. Collection laws – Canada. I. Title.

HG3752.7.C3S54 2009   658.8'80971   C2009–903893–5

We acknowledge the financial support of the Government of Canada through the Book Publishing Industry Development Program and that of the Government of Ontario through the Ontario Media Development Corporation's Ontario Book Initiative. We further acknowledge the support of the Canada Council for the Arts and the Ontario Arts Council for our publishing program.

Typeset in Garamond by M&S, Toronto
Printed and bound in Canada

The purpose of this book is to educate and assist Canadians who are receiving collection calls or who are experiencing significant challenges with their debts. It is not intended to be legal advice. This book is sold on the understanding that the author is not acting as the lawyer for the reader, and the advice herein should not be construed as legal advice. Any person reading this book seeking legal advice should speak to a lawyer and seek advice appropriate for his or her particular situation.

 ANCIENT FOREST
FRIENDLY

This book is printed on ancient-forest friendly paper.

McClelland & Stewart Ltd.
75 Sherbourne Street
Toronto, Ontario
M5A 2P9
www.mcclelland.com

1   2   3   4   5   14   13   12   11   10

CONTENTS

Appendices

INTRODUCTION

If you're reading this book you're probably experiencing serious debt problems. Maybe you've been having trouble making the minimum monthly payments on your credit cards. Maybe your utility bills are mounting and you just can't pay them any more. You might already be receiving bothersome collection calls about your overdue bills, and if not, you might soon because you're getting buried under them. People run into debt problems for all sorts of reasons: you might have recently lost your job or are earning less than you used to, or maybe you or your family has health issues, or your expenses have gone up because of a divorce, a separation, or the end of a common-law relationship. Whatever the cause, this is probably a tough time in your life, and you may be feeling anxious and afraid about what the future may bring.

Let me assure you: you are not alone.

Today more than a million Canadians are facing serious debt problems, and things have become much worse since the fall of 2008, when the world's economy fell off a cliff. For example, the number of personal bankruptcies in May 2009 was 31 per cent higher than in the previous May. Almost every day I receive telephone calls from Canadians who used to enjoy a comfortable lifestyle but who now worry about going bankrupt because their household income is less than it was two years ago, their credit card interest rates have gone up, or they have little or no equity in their home.

This is a situation I'm all too familiar with. I'm trained as a lawyer, and from 1994 to 2006 I worked almost exclusively on behalf of collection agencies, helping them recover tens of millions of dollars from consumers like you. My law office was located right on the collection floor at some of the largest agencies in the country. In many cases, anywhere between 50 and 200 collectors would be sitting at workstations just a few steps from my office door. I dealt with various agency employees – owners, senior management, collection supervisors, and collectors, as well as customer service, human resources, accounting, and IT – on virtually a daily basis. I would take coffee breaks and have lunch with these people. I like to think that some of them were, and even today are, my friends.

During that period, I sent out my share of collection letters to consumers across Canada, and my law firm also employed as many as 30 legal assistants who spent most of their days making collection calls. At some point in the past maybe *you* received a letter or phone call from my law firm demanding payment of an outstanding account. Apart from doing collections, my experience also includes managing a collection agency's legal department, reviewing contracts with creditors, defending collection agencies in lawsuits, and responding to complaints brought against them.

Over time I became increasingly uncomfortable with how I earned a living, and in 2007 I decided to stop representing collection agencies and stop doing debt collection work. After a few months of soul-searching, I came to the conclusion that I might be able to earn a living providing advice and assistance to consumers who had debt problems instead. Over the next several months I began reorienting my two law practices (in Ontario and New York state) toward helping consumers. I now have clients in virtually every province. I have found my niche in the world, I enjoy my work, and I sleep very well at night.

After I switched sides, I also started writing this book. My goal in doing so is to give you practical advice that you won't find in one place anywhere else. *The Wolf at the Door* will show you how to stop, avoid, or discourage collection calls. It also describes the debt collection process and your eight options for dealing with debt, which should help you make better decisions in this area. Things are probably not as bleak as you think! Even if you owe enormous sums to various creditors, you might be able to extricate yourself from your current financial hole. Finally, this book should bring you some peace of mind, and depending upon your particular financial situation, might save you money – in some cases even thousands of dollars.

The book is written based on my personal experience acting as a collection lawyer and with input from a number of senior people currently working in the collection industry. I have also conducted extensive interviews with bankruptcy trustees and front-line counsellors at credit counselling agencies and firms providing debt settlement and debt consulting services. Unfortunately, too few of these individuals fully appreciate the entire range of solutions available to you in dealing with your debts, and they don't always offer unbiased information about *all* of your options. I will explain all of them, helping you make informed decisions and do what's best for you and your family.

Part One of this book, "So You're Having Financial Problems," gives background information about how creditors attempt to collect your debt – it helps you know your opponent. You will be introduced to those individuals demanding money from you: collectors employed by your creditor or a collection agency, and law firms. Part Two, "How to Stop, Avoid, or Discourage Collection Calls," explains how to deal with collection calls. Part Three, "How to Avoid Paying Your Outstanding Accounts," explains the various reasons that you might not have to pay your bills. Part Four, "How to Resolve Your Outstanding Debts and Protect Your Credit Rating," outlines your options for handling your accounts, and Part Five, "How to Deal with Unprofessional Bill Collectors," covers what to do if a collector is behaving inappropriately in his dealings with you.

Collection agencies, especially the larger ones, are able to draw on tremendous resources in their attempts to collect money from you. Some collection agencies have state-of-the-art call centres, often employing hundreds of collectors and using sophisticated computer and telephone equipment – operations worth millions of dollars. The collector phoning you will have gone through some kind of training program, may have been employed for several years as a collector, and has access to the shared wisdom of the management team at her place of employment. In contrast, you likely have little experience, knowledge, and resources to deal with their calls.

Debt collection is a serious matter, and owing money to your creditors can have serious consequences, but to help you understand what is taking place, I find it useful to describe the process as a game. Personally, I like to watch a sporting event between two evenly matched opponents. When you read this book, you might think of me as the coach for your team, one who used to play for the opposition. Your creditor's team is wearing the black jerseys. Your team is wearing the white jerseys and includes your household members, family, and possibly some kind of agent, a debt settlement firm, a lawyer, or even a credit counselling agency. If you read this book carefully, understand it, and apply what you have learned, my hope is that you will find the playing field between you and your collectors levelled and that you will be able to win the contest with your creditors.

PART ONE

SO YOU'RE HAVING FINANCIAL PROBLEMS

Before learning about how to dig yourself out of your financial hole, it is important for you to understand certain background information about the debt collection process and about your credit score, that all-important number that determines if you can borrow money and at what cost. In Chapter 1, "The Basics of the Debt Collection Game," I will introduce you to the key players in the debt collection process and explain the life cycle of an outstanding account. In Chapter 2, "What You Should Know About Your Credit Report and Your Credit Score," I will cover the basics of consumer credit.

THE BASICS OF THE DEBT COLLECTION GAME

Before we get into what to do if you're being hounded by collection agencies or if you're drowning in debt, it's important that you understand some of the basics of how debt collection works. This chapter will give you an overview of the process and introduce you to some of the key players.

PRACTICAL TIP

This book will introduce a number of words and phrases you might be unfamiliar with. I will explain them as I go along, and the glossary at the back also defines each term.

As you may know all too well, *collectors* are the people who call you and call you and call you. They are usually very aggressive and they want you to make a payment as soon as possible. A *creditor* is a company from which you purchased goods or services, or from which you borrowed money, such as Visa. A *debtor* or *consumer* is the person who owes the money: you.

A *bill collector* is an individual or an organization demanding payment from debtors – for example, your creditor, a collection agency, a lawyer, or one of its employees. A *collection agency* is an organization that collects money from you *on behalf of others* and obtains at least 50 per cent of its revenues from this collection work, such as a traditional collection agency or a law firm that does large-volume debt collection work. We will learn more about bill collectors later in this chapter, but the important thing for you to understand here is that they are not always employed by collection agencies.

If collection agencies are calling you, it's probably about *unsecured debt.* This is debt for which your creditor has no collateral if you do not pay it, which is why they're more likely to send those accounts to collections. The most common types of unsecured debts are most credit cards; certain debt typically worth less than $10,000 such as bank overdrafts, lines of credit, and personal loans; certain utilities such as your telephone landline, cellphone, Internet, and cable television subscription; student loans; and outstanding taxes.

With a *secured debt* your creditor has collateral that it can turn to if you fail to repay your account. A good example of a secured debt is a loan you take out to lease or purchase a car. The lender usually puts a lien on the vehicle, making your car the collateral, so that if you fail to make your payments your lender can repossess your car. Similarly, when you purchase a home, your lender puts a mortgage on your property. The property is the lender's collateral, and if you fail to make your mortgage payments your lender may take steps to repossess your property. Lenders usually insist on becoming a secured creditor for large personal loans or lines of credit.

Consumer debt includes debt arising from the purchase of goods and services or from borrowing money from a lender other than the government. The following are *not* consumer debt: unpaid child support and spousal support, and money owing to the government such as unpaid income taxes and property taxes, fines, and outstanding student loans (except Canada Student Loans obtained between August 1, 1995, and July 31, 2000, in which case your creditor is a financial institution and not the Government of Canada).

IMPORTANT FACT
This book is going to be most valuable in helping you deal with your unsecured consumer debt (credit card bills, for example).

In order to deal with your debt situation effectively, you need to be able to identify which of your debts are unsecured consumer debts. One of the things you need to know is whether you have signed a *Master Credit Agreement* with your financial institution. Without fanfare, over the past several years the banking industry has been quietly reducing its exposure to bad loans on unsecured debt by getting both new and existing customers to sign a Master Credit Agreement. Under the agreement, the financial institution makes a certain amount of credit available to a customer and the customer agrees to provide collateral for this debt – making it secured debt. In most cases the security a banking customer provides is his property – his home, townhouse, or condominium. Many people unwittingly signed these agreements without understanding that they effectively converted some of their existing unsecured debt into secured debt. If you are unsure whether you have signed a Master Credit Agreement with a particular financial institution, you should ask for documentation regarding your loans or sources of credit.

Once you've figured out if any of your debts fall under a Master Credit Agreement, you might take five or ten minutes to list all of them in Appendix A: "Worksheet: Profile of Your Current Debts." This will help you to keep track of, categorize, and identify your unsecured consumer debts, those you might be able to avoid paying altogether through something called a limitation period or that you might be able to settle for less than 100 cents on the dollar. As we'll discuss, it is possible to negotiate incredible deals with some creditors that allow you to eliminate your debt at huge discounts. I spend the majority of my time as a lawyer doing this for my clients. For instance, I have helped clients who owe more than $25,000 to a certain creditor eliminate their debt for less than $5,000.

Some other terms you'll come across in the book relate to this practice. A *settlement* occurs when a creditor accepts one or more payments for less than 100 per cent of the amount owing as *settlement in full.* This is in contrast to *payment in full,* whereby a consumer resolves an outstanding account by paying 100 per cent of the outstanding balance. The vast majority of settlements involve a *lump sum payment,* which is a single payment, versus *instalment payments,* which happen over a period of time, usually with post-dated cheques.

This book contains references to *real property* and *personal property.* Real property, also called real estate, includes a house, townhouse, condominium, farm, cottage, or rental property. Any property that is not real property would typically be described as personal property. A car, mobile home, and whatever is not permanently attached to the walls, floors, or ceiling in your residence is personal property.

WHAT YOU SHOULD KNOW
ABOUT GOVERNMENT DEBTS

Although the primary focus of this book is how to deal with unsecured consumer debt, many Canadians also owe money to the government, such as the following:

- income tax
- certain Canada Student Loans
- provincial student loans
- government fines, including parking tickets
- overpayment of government benefits
- property taxes

- statutory payroll deductions, provincial sales tax, or GST, if you're a sole proprietor of a business

Before we continue, I should say a word about this kind of debt, because there are some special considerations you should be aware of when you owe money to the government. First, the government typically attempts to recover 100 per cent of the money owing to it – plus interest and penalties – and is unlikely to agree to settlements of less than 100 cents on the dollar. However, it might be possible to negotiate settlements on provincial student loans. And if you obtained a Canada Student Loan between August 1, 1995, and July 31, 2000, your creditor is a private lender, not the Government of Canada, so may agree to a settlement.

Special Powers Available to the Federal Government to Collect a Debt

The federal government has a number of tools to collect a debt that are not available to any other creditor. Some of my clients have learned about these the hard way.

Jim went to his neighbourhood bank branch to deposit his paycheque, pay some bills, and withdraw some cash. The teller informed Jim that he would be back in a minute. Jim observed the teller speaking to his supervisor. When the teller returned, Jim was informed that his account had been "frozen." Jim was shocked. He then spoke to the supervisor and was given the name and phone number of someone at Canada Revenue Agency (CRA). When Jim phoned the CRA, the representative told him that his bank account had been frozen in connection with personal income tax that he owed.

In this situation the Canada Revenue Agency *issued a requirement to pay,* a collection tool the federal government can use against anyone who owes money to it. Most commonly it will issue a requirement to pay to your financial institution, effectively freezing your bank accounts, but if you have a tenant in your home, it could also instruct your tenant to make her rental payments to it instead of to you.

In May of last year, Bill, a recent university graduate, was expecting a nice income tax refund of about $2,500 from the CRA. When Bill received his Notice of Assessment from the CRA he was surprised to learn that he was not going to receive a refund after all because the federal government had clawed it back to help pay off his outstanding Canada Student Loan. The federal government had exercised a statutory right of set-off.

What You Should Know About Canada Student Loans

There is a lot of confusion among Canadians about their outstanding student loans. This section is not intended to be a comprehensive review of student loans, but it will highlight some of the important issues when dealing with them. First, note that Quebec, Nunavut, and the Northwest Territories do not participate in the Canada Student Loan program. These jurisdictions receive money from the federal government and operate their own assistance programs for students.

A person who obtains a Canada Student Loan will typically also obtain a provincial student loan. If you have a Canada Student Loan you have an obligation to begin repaying it six months after completion of your post-secondary studies, although interest will be charged from the beginning of this six-month grace period. Under the Canada Student Loan program a borrower is considered to be in default when his loan is more than three months in arrears, and it will undertake some collection efforts at that point.

If you have delinquent student loans, one of the first things you will want to do is determine how many delinquent student loans you have and who the collection agent is for each of these loans. Your primary point of contact regarding your Canada Student

Loan should be the National Student Loans Service Centre (NSLSC). Its website is www.canlearn.ca. The centre has two separate divisions, one for students attending public universities and community colleges and one for students attending trade schools, career colleges, and vocational schools. You can also get information about provincial student loans obtained in Ontario, Saskatchewan, Newfoundland and Labrador, or New Brunswick from the National Student Loans Service Centre.

IMPORTANT FACT
Whenever you are dealing with the National Student Loans Service Centre or an authorized collection agent, it is important that you maintain a written journal summarizing your communications with them, that you retain copies of any correspondence with them, and that they confirm receipt of any written communications from you.

Relief from Canada Student Loans
If you have a Canada Student Loan that you are experiencing difficulty repaying, you might be eligible for various forms of relief, including these:

1. Revision of Terms: A borrower decreases or increases the monthly loan payments or extends the number of months she takes to repay her Canada Student Loan.
2. Interest Relief: A borrower who is experiencing short-term difficulties repaying his student loan is not required to make any interest or principal payments for a period of six months.
3. Debt Reduction in Repayment: A borrower experiencing long-term financial problems might be able to reduce her monthly loan payments to an amount she can afford based on her income.
4. Permanent Disability or Death Benefit: If a borrower dies or becomes permanently disabled, his Canada Student Loan might be forgiven.

Anyone wishing to take advantage of these relief options must apply for them, and may or may not be successful. Similar relief may be available under provincial student loan programs.

THE LIFE CYCLE OF AN OVERDUE DEBT

Let's say the minimum payment for your MasterCard is due February 10, 2010, and you don't pay it. Your account is now considered in default. Most creditors employ their own collectors who will attempt to collect a debt for anywhere between three and six months from the date you first default on your payments.

If the creditor's collectors are unsuccessful getting you to pay, the creditor will typically send your account to a collection agency. A collection agency makes money on a commission basis – so the creditor pays it only when you make a payment. This commission is a percentage of the money the agency collects – the rates vary anywhere between 8 per cent and 60 per cent – and typically the longer your account goes unpaid, the higher the commission rate. For example, if you make a $1,000 payment to a collection agency toward your ABC Mart credit card debt and the collection agency is entitled to a 30 per cent commission, it will keep $300.

IMPORTANT FACT

A creditor will place your outstanding account with only one collection agency at a time.

The first time your delinquent account is assigned to a collection agency, your account is considered a *first assign*. At this point some of your creditors might stop charging you interest. Your account will be with this agency for a predetermined period of time, usually between 6 and 12 months. Either one specific collector will be working your account or it will be worked by a group of collectors. It is more likely to be worked by a single collector if it is worth more than $400 and is less than six months in default.

If the collection agency is unsuccessful getting you to make a payment, the creditor will take back your account from this original agency and forward it to a new one, making your account a *second assign*.

If you still don't pay, your creditor may forward your overdue account to several collection agencies, but again only one collection agency at a time. These are called *third assigns* or in some cases even *fourth assigns*. It is possible for your account to be a third assign even when it has been a third assign at several different collection agencies.

At some point your creditor might simply write off your unpaid account or sell it to a *debt buyer* or *debt purchaser*. That usually happens when the debt is more than three years old, although these days more and more creditors are selling debt earlier. A debt buyer steps into the shoes of your original creditor, replacing it. So if you owe $500 on your Bay credit card and this debt is sold to ACME Debt Buyers USA, then you now owe this debt to ACME Debt Buyers USA.

There are two different categories of debt buyers: traditional collection agencies and debt purchasing firms that specialize in buying a large number of delinquent accounts from a single creditor. For example, a collection agency might purchase 10,000 accounts from a department store credit card issuer, paying between half a cent and five cents for each dollar of debt. Now when the collection agency collects $1,000 from you, it keeps 100 per cent, rather than just a commission. Specialized debt buying firms, on the other hand, will typically send the accounts they purchase to a collection agency for collection on a commission basis, but a few debt buyers actually employ their own collectors.

Somewhere between 50 per cent and 75 per cent of the outstanding consumer debt in Canada is owed to the big Canadian chartered banks, which have been very reluctant to sell any of their debt. Given how much they value their reputations and given how some collection agencies treat people in debt, I am not in the least surprised.

And finally, after a certain period of time, you might be able to avoid paying some of your debts altogether. Every Canadian province and territory has what is known as a *statute of limitations*. Depending upon which province you live in, the limitation period on a consumer debt might expire between two and six years from the date of your last payment. After the expiry of a limitation period, you will have the option of not paying your outstanding account and your creditor will have effectively lost its ability to recover the money from you. We will learn more about this later, and about how you might be able to use the limitation period to your advantage.

WHO ARE THESE PEOPLE CALLING YOU?

A lot of people tell me they are confused about who is actually contacting them to demand payment of their outstanding account. In the next few pages I will introduce you to the various people you may come across.

Collectors employed by a creditor

For the first three to six months that your account is overdue, you will likely receive calls from collectors employed by your creditor. Because I represent debtors, I routinely get calls from these collectors myself, and many of them are so rude to me that I can only imagine how rude they are to my clients. I got so mad one day after a call from a collector named Gary that I decided to start recording my phone calls with certain collectors so I could post them on my firm's website, www.helpwithcollectioncalls.ca. (Unfortunately, Gary never did call me back.) The problem is, except in British Columbia, there are virtually no laws other than the Criminal Code protecting consumers from the bad behaviour of a collector employed by your creditor. They aren't held to the same code of conduct as collectors employed by collection agencies. So when my clients complain about getting abusive phone calls from collection agencies, in many cases I believe they are mistaken and in fact the caller was a collector employed by their creditor.

If you owe money to a finance company, the local branch manager might be knocking on your door demanding payment. There are no laws prohibiting a creditor from doing this, whereas most provinces do have laws prohibiting employees *of a collection agency* from showing up at your residence to demand payment of a debt. Collection agencies are limited to phoning you and sending you letters demanding payment of an outstanding account.

Furthermore, collectors employed by creditors often will not provide you with their first and last names, possibly because anonymity helps them avoid getting in trouble for abusive or unprofessional behaviour. In contrast, most provincial laws regulating collection agencies require individual collectors to be licensed and to disclose their full name during a collection call, once they have confirmed that they are speaking with a debtor.

Collectors employed by a collection agency
I am a regular guest on a consumer advocacy radio show in Toronto, and often people calling in want to learn more about the kind of person who works as a collection agency collector. I describe the job as similar to commission sales, because most collectors are paid a base salary, plus a bonus or commission. A good collector can make thousands of dollars in bonuses in a month. However, a collector who is having a bad month can find himself fired. Collectors are under tremendous pressure to collect money and this encourages them to engage in bad behaviour.

Collectors typically have to be at least 19 years old. About 40 per cent are women. There are no educational requirements whatsoever to be a collector.

During my 12 years as a collection lawyer, I came to know hundreds of collectors working at collection agencies. Many of these people are no different from you and me, or your co-workers, and believe it or not many of them are decent people doing a very difficult job. If you are in serious debt, some of these collectors will even connect you with lenders they know so you can get a debt consolidation loan, enabling you to reduce your monthly payments on your existing debt. A few years ago one of my legal assistants showed me a thank you letter she had received from a consumer expressing appreciation for her assistance with resolving an outstanding account.

Having said that, collection agencies employ far too many collectors who are unprofessional, unethical, and mean-spirited and who break the law on a regular basis. A few very successful collectors have even filed for personal bankruptcy themselves or have a criminal record for serious offences.

Furthermore, collectors know how the debt collection process operates, and you might be surprised to learn that some of them work the system to avoid paying their own debts. They know that "Creditor X" will settle a delinquent account for 50 cents on the dollar after 24 months. Similarly, they know that "Creditor Y" never sues anyone, so they will not pay "Creditor Y" and simply wait for a limitation period to expire so they can avoid paying that debt altogether. Several years ago when I was doing collection work, I approached a collection agency near Burlington, Ontario, proposing that it let me try to collect 200 accounts they were unsuccessful with, as a test of my abilities. Imagine my surprise, and that of the agency's management, when I discovered that one of these delinquent accounts belonged to *one of its own collectors.*

There are two scenarios in which you will receive a telephone call from a collector working at a collection agency. In the traditional scenario, collectors working a "desk" or a "queue" are assigned to work a specific group of accounts and they will manually dial these debtors' phone numbers. The older the accounts, the more accounts a collector working a desk may have. A collector might work 75 to 100 accounts a month on first assigns, over 200 accounts a month on second assigns, and as many as 450 accounts on third assigns. A collector working a desk will usually work a specific group of files for a few months before the accounts are transferred to a different collector. If you are receiving calls from a collector working a desk, you will likely receive several calls from the same collector over a number of weeks or months.

You might be receiving automated computer-generated calls from a collection agency that is using an expensive piece of hardware known as a *dialer.* By using a dialer a collection agency can dial thousands of phone numbers in a few hours. If the agency is using an unsophisticated dialer, the recipient will simply receive a pre-recorded message requesting a return call to a particular phone number regarding an important matter. This pre-recorded message will never mention the name of the collection agency, due to laws against disclosing the existence of a debt to anyone but the debtor. If the collection agency is using a sophisticated dialer, when an outbound call is answered by an actual person, the call is immediately transferred to a collector who works in a group of collectors, who will be able to access the file corresponding to the phone number. If you are receiving phone calls from a collection agency using a sophisticated dialer, you might end up speaking to several different collectors during a relatively short period of time.

A collector, regardless of whether she is working a "desk" or on a dialer, may at some point have you speak to another collector, typically a more experienced one with a proven track record of obtaining voluntary payments. This is referred to as a *double.* Collection agencies use doubles to reinforce the importance of making a payment or meeting a payment deadline.

Lawyers who do debt collection work

You might get confused if you are receiving collection letters or calls from your original creditor or a collection agency and then you get a letter from a lawyer. It is common for both creditors and collection agencies to hire lawyers to send out large numbers of letters demanding payment of a debt on the lawyer's letterhead – and often the lawyer has no real involvement other than that.

A handful of Canadian law practices operate in a very similar fashion to a collection agency. These law firms collect large numbers of consumer accounts, employing staff whose primary function is to make collection calls. Many of these employees previously worked as collectors with a collection agency. The trouble is, a lawyer's conduct is regulated by provincial law societies, so they face few restrictions when doing collections work, except in British Columbia. For example, there is one law firm that would probably rank between the 20th- and 25th-largest collection agency in Canada, based on revenues. This lawyer's office may send out as many as 150,000 collection letters to consumers each year.

Some lawyers engaged in debt collection work in Canada employ collection techniques that would be illegal if done by a collection agency. A prime example of this is sending what is known in the collection industry as a *draft statement of claim*, which I would describe as a lawyer's demand letter on steroids. Basically, it's a notice saying that a lawyer has prepared the paperwork necessary to commence a lawsuit, and if the consumer doesn't pay his account within ten business days, he will be sued. Furthermore, the letter contains a form identical to what a creditor would use to sue a debtor in Ontario Small Claims Court. Provincial laws prohibit collection agencies, but not lawyers, from using an imitation court form when collecting a debt.

UNDERSTAND THEIR TACTICS

Keep in mind that the collector calling you is getting paid to recover money from you, and the more she collects the more money she makes. A collector's job is not to call you and discuss the weather or the score from last night's hockey game. The collector's job is to make you feel uncomfortable, to motivate you to act, and to get you to resolve your account as soon as possible. Collectors are trained to do this. Collectors want you to believe that there will be negative consequences if you do not pay your outstanding account. They want to create a sense of urgency, to make you feel that the debt you owe to their employer's client has to be paid in the immediate future, before you pay some of your other bills.

One of the most effective ways for a collector to persuade someone to pay a debt is to humiliate him during a collection call. Most of the tactics a collector may employ to humiliate you are illegal. Some might call you a deadbeat or a loser. They might threaten to speak to your boss or the human resources department where you work. The collector is sending the message "I am going to make your life hell until you find the money to pay this account." A collector might also try to appeal to your personal ethics: your honesty and your sense of fair play. The collector might get you to admit that you owe the money and that you do have a moral obligation to repay the debt. If you only knew how dishonest some of these collectors were themselves, you would laugh at the irony of their playing this card.

A collector might also make less emotional appeals, such as advising you that failure to pay within four business days will result in a lawsuit. It is important for you to know that the collector is a low-level employee who has no authority to authorize a lawsuit. A collector might get chewed out by her supervisor for being away from her workstation for more than 15 minutes without permission. Any deadline she gives you regarding a lawsuit is just some date she has picked out of thin air and is meaningless.

Recently, two senior executives at some of Canada's largest collection agencies shared a surprising revelation with me. Most, if not all, of Canada's chartered banks do not give collection agencies prior approval to sue files when they forward their thousands of outstanding accounts. This means that collection agencies working on behalf of major banks must usually seek the client's permission to sue a particular file. Given the banks' procedure for suing files, it is doubtful that a collection agency would even request permission to sue in the first place.

Large creditors, including chartered banks, credit card issuers, major retailers, and utilities, determine early on whether they are interested in suing a file. If your outstanding account is sent to a collection agency as a first assign, this almost guarantees that you are not going to be sued, especially if your original creditor owns the debt. My best guess is that Canadian collection agencies as a whole sue fewer than one in 10,000 accounts on behalf of major creditors. When you get your first notice or call from a collection agency, particularly if your debt is owed to a large creditor, you might want to go out and celebrate because this means the odds are remote that your creditor intends to sue you. And in many respects, a collection agency and its collectors are impotent unless they are going to sue you.

Your odds of being sued are also slim to none if you owe less than $5,000 to a particular creditor, you support yourself on social assistance, your account has been purchased by a debt buyer, or you do not own real estate in your own name and you live in New Brunswick, where garnishments are not available to creditors. Furthermore, your odds of being sued approach zero if you do not own your own home and you have a low-wage job.

IMPORTANT FACT

In Canada creditors, collection agencies, and collection lawyers routinely threaten to sue consumers when they never have any intention of doing so.

Despite all of that, it is very common for creditors, collection agencies, or collection lawyers to threaten to sue you if you do not pay your debt within a few days. In the United States this practice is illegal and you could actually sue a collection agency or a law firm for thousands of dollars for doing it. But in Canada it is perfectly legal for them to threaten you with a lawsuit even when they don't intend to.

IMPORTANT FACT

Collectors often make false or misleading statements to debtors, which is an illegal practice.

It is very common for collectors to suggest that you will face other dire consequences if you fail to pay your account in the immediate future. Ontario-based collectors often threaten that they will send a bailiff or Sheriff to a consumer's residence next week to seize his personal property if he does not pay his debt within 48 hours. They don't have the authority to do this without a judgment, which they can obtain only after successfully suing you, so it's an empty threat. One Ontario collector proudly told me the story of how he telephoned a consumer's wife one morning and told her to put all the couple's furniture and home electronics equipment out on the front lawn because the Sheriff would be coming by at 5 p.m. to repossess it. Her husband was humiliated when he came home from work that evening only to discover their television, stereo, and living room furniture sitting on the front lawn.

My point here is that if you're feeling intimidated by collection calls, try to maintain calm, because the collector doesn't have nearly as much power as you might think.

PROTECT YOUR FINANCES FROM SEIZURE

I'll end this chapter with an important word of caution: you should be using more than one financial institution. More than half of Canadians do all their banking at just one bank, trust company, or credit union. Ideally, you should avoid having your chequing account, savings account, and RRSP at the same financial institution where you have your mortgage, personal loan, line of credit, or credit card. If you owe money to your bank on a credit card, bank overdraft, personal loan, or line of credit, it might exercise what's called a *right of set-off* and seize money from your savings or chequing accounts – without notice – and apply these amounts against your debt. Financial institutions recover significant amounts of money on a regular basis exercising this right of set-off against their customers.

CHAPTER 2

WHAT YOU SHOULD KNOW ABOUT YOUR CREDIT SCORE AND YOUR CREDIT REPORT

When you go to rent an apartment, or apply for a credit card, line of credit, bank overdraft, car loan, or mortgage, your prospective lender wants to know the likelihood that it will be repaid.

A *credit reporting agency* is a company that provides its members, fee-paying creditors, with information regarding the creditworthiness of consumers. The two major credit reporting agencies in Canada are TransUnion and Equifax. Your ability to borrow money or obtain credit is based on their assessment.

Most large creditors are members of both TransUnion and Equifax. It is possible that your creditor is a member of only one, in which case your account will appear with either TransUnion or Equifax, but not both. Some smaller creditors may simply not be members of credit reporting agencies and not list any information whatsoever on your credit report.

These credit reporting agencies are for-profit companies that receive payments from their members and they serve the needs of their members. Contrary to what you might think, credit reporting agencies are not government agencies, nor is it their mandate to serve the public. Some provinces, but not all, have a law regulating the conduct of credit reporting agencies.

YOUR CREDIT SCORE

TransUnion and Equifax use a credit score to rate your credit-worthiness. Your *credit score* is a number between 300 and 900. Your *Beacon Score* is the name used by Equifax for its credit score. TransUnion refers to its credit score as an *Empirica Score.* Your credit score at TransUnion might be a different number from your credit score at Equifax.

The higher your credit score, the more you are considered a good credit risk. Prospective lenders and credit grantors will look at your credit score when determining whether to approve or decline your application for credit. In addition, based on your credit score individual lenders will place you into a particular category of risk. Those people falling into a higher-risk class will pay a higher interest rate. Similarly, those who are in a low-risk class will pay a much lower interest rate.

A number of factors are taken into consideration in determining your credit score, including the following:

1. Repayment history, including your credit rating on various accounts
2. Current debt level
3. Credit applications and inquiries
4. Age and marital status
5. Home ownership
6. Your occupation and your employment stability
7. Length of time at your current residence

You will have to pay a fee to obtain your credit score from TransUnion or Equifax. The easiest way to do so is to visit www.equifax.ca or www.transunion.ca, pay a fee using a credit card, and obtain your credit score online.

YOUR CREDIT REPORT

Your *credit report*, sometimes called a *credit bureau*, is a document you obtain from a credit reporting agency. Your credit score might not appear on your credit report. Your credit report lists some, but perhaps not all, of your creditors, the amounts your creditors say is owing, and how current you are on these obligations. Your credit report might also reveal any judgments against you. Not all creditors report money owed to them on a credit report. Financial institutions, for example, do not report mortgage obligations on a credit report.

PRACTICAL TIP

If a debt doesn't appear on your credit report, for all intents and purposes, it doesn't exist, which may be an excellent reason not to pay it.

A *credit rating* is a number assigned to each item that appears on your credit report, between R1 and R9 (there is no such thing as an R6 or an R8). These numbers mean the following:

R0   Too new for creditor to rate

R1   Consumer is current on his obligations

R2   Consumer is one payment late (30 to 60 days overdue)

R3   Consumer is two payments late (60 to 90 days overdue)

R4   Consumer is three payments late (90 to 120 days overdue)

R5   Consumer is four payments late (a minimum of 120 days overdue)

R7   Consumer is making payments under a debt management plan with a credit counselling agency

R9   Creditor has written the account off as a bad debt (150 to 180 days overdue)

Once your account is six months in arrears, it will typically become an R9, be written off as a bad debt, and be sent to a collection agency for collection. One or more R9s on your credit report will lower your credit score. When a consumer has filed for personal bankruptcy, her accounts will usually be listed as an R9. Once a consumer is discharged from bankruptcy any accounts discharged should be removed from the report; however, it will show that the consumer has filed for bankruptcy.

Collectors may tell you it is important to pay your account immediately if you want to protect your credit rating. This statement may have some validity if your account is less than six months in default and none of your other accounts are R9s. However, many creditors do not send their outstanding accounts to a collection agency until a debt is six months in default and the account is already an R9. If you have accounts that are six months in default, you can likely afford to take the next few months, or possibly years, to resolve your outstanding debts on terms favourable to you.

Collectors and collection agencies often suggest that your repayment history is the only factor prospective lenders consider when making a loan or providing credit. In fact, your repayment history may count for just 30 per cent in determining your credit score. You might still be able to borrow money if you have a spotty repayment history, or you might be unable to borrow a nickel even if you had a perfect record making payments to your creditors. Some of my new clients will tell me they have an excellent credit rating because they have never missed a payment. When I ask them if they have been able to borrow money to pay their debts, they tell me they cannot, because they owe too much to their creditors. In fact, these individuals probably have a poor credit score because of the amount of their debt.

The vast majority of information that credit reporting agencies receive about you comes directly from their members, your creditors. Creditors provide this information to credit reporting agencies electronically once a month. However, sometimes large creditors will delegate to collection agencies the responsibility of providing TransUnion and Equifax with information regarding any payments you make to an agency. Unfortunately, some collection agencies have a reputation for not doing a very thorough job of updating consumers' credit reports after payments are made.

The information on your credit report is only as good as the information your creditors, or in some cases collection agencies, provide to a credit reporting agency. It is prudent for you to review your credit report every six months so you can detect inaccurate information, fraud, or identity theft, or a creditor's failure to update it after you made a payment in full or settled an outstanding account.

PRACTICAL TIP
If you discover you have been the victim of fraud or identity theft, immediately inform the police, obtain a copy of the police report, and send copies of it to the relevant creditors, their authorized collection agents, and TransUnion and Equifax.

Problems will arise if you claim you have been the victim of identity theft or fraud and you do not provide your creditor with a copy of a police report. For example, if your son uses your credit card and forges your signature to make a credit card purchase and you do not report it, your creditor will hold you liable for the purchase.

Obtaining your credit report from Equifax
There are a variety of ways you can obtain a copy of your credit report from Equifax (it will be free if you request it by telephone, by mail, or by fax, but you will have to pay a fee to get it online):

1. By telephone by calling 1-800-465-7166.
   By mailing your request to:
   Equifax Canada Inc.
   Box 190 Jean Talon Station
   Montreal, PQ, H1S 2Z2

2. By faxing your request to (514) 355-8502.
3. Online at www.equifax.ca. You will need to make a credit
   card payment of $15.50. You can obtain online access to
   both your credit report *and* your Equifax credit score by
   making a $23.95 online payment.

I would recommend that you obtain a copy of your credit report online, which will require just a credit card payment. If you request your report by fax or mail, you will have to provide photocopies of two pieces of identification, such as your driver's licence, social insurance number, or passport, or possibly a utility bill with your name on it.

In addition to your credit report, you can also obtain your credit score from Equifax and subscribe to a credit monitoring service under which you are notified of any important changes to your credit profile.

Obtaining your credit report from TransUnion
You can obtain a copy of your credit report from TransUnion online at www.transunion.ca. It costs $14.95.

If you want to obtain a free copy of your credit report by mail, you will have to download the Consumer Disclosure form from the TransUnion website. After completing the form, mail it, together with two pieces of satisfactory identification, to:

TransUnion Consumer Relations Centre
P.O. Box 338, LCD1
Hamilton, ON, L8L 7W2

You can also sign up on www.transunion.ca for a monthly credit monitoring service for $14.95 a month.

Updating your credit report

If you have paid your outstanding account, you will want to obtain a release letter from the collection agency. You should request this ten business days after you make your final payment to the collection agency.

When you finalize your account, the update might take 60 or 90 days to show up on your credit report. If there is some urgency for your credit report to show that you have resolved an outstanding account – for example, if you wish to obtain a mortgage – you can try contacting the Customer Service Department at the collection agency. Inform the employee that you resolved your account but your credit report has yet to be updated. You can request his assistance in contacting the credit reporting agency to update your credit report or in contacting your creditor to have it update your credit report.

You could also contact Equifax and/or TransUnion yourself. Ask your lender if you need to get the account updated on your credit reports at both Equifax or TransUnion or just one. If Equifax or TransUnion has an office near you, you might find it helpful to go in person with two pieces of satisfactory ID, a copy of your release letter, and if applicable, a copy of a receipt and your settlement letter (documents we describe in detail in Chapter 21, "Tips for Making a Payment on Your Debt"). If you show the staff these documents you might be able to get your credit report updated more quickly.

How long does information remain on your credit report?

IMPORTANT FACT

Any information on your credit report about a delinquent account should be removed six years from the date of last payment.

There is some variation in provincial law as well as in the company policy of Equifax and TransUnion regarding how long an item will remain on your credit report. A person's first bankruptcy will likely appear on her credit report for six years. A second bankruptcy might appear on a person's credit report for 12 years. In the case of a consumer's third bankruptcy, the bankruptcy will never be removed from the consumer's credit report.

PART TWO

HOW TO STOP, AVOID, OR DISCOURAGE COLLECTION CALLS

You may be receiving collection calls from someone demanding that you pay a debt. Or you may be getting automated messages requesting a return call. These calls may run the spectrum from innocuous to annoying, to upsetting, to so outrageous that you want to call the police. I receive phone calls on a regular basis from people who complain about bill collectors trying to humiliate them or scare them with threats of imminent repossession of property, garnishment of wages, threats to disclose the existence of the debt to their employer, and in some cases even jail or deportation. They phone me because they are looking for help. They want these calls to stop. In this section, I answer this cry for help.

Under Canadian law, a bill collector's right to communicate with a debtor is not absolute. There are restrictions on what they can do. For example, each Canadian province and territory has a law prohibiting collection agencies from calling you during certain hours of the day and certain days of the year (see Appendix B, "Times When Collection Calls Are Prohibited"). In Part Two, I will explain the various things you can do to avoid unwanted collection calls.

In Chapter 3, I explain your right to *stop* collection calls. Unfortunately, depending on which province or territory you live in, you may not be in a position to stop a bill collector from calling you. Accordingly, in Chapter 4 I provide practical advice for *avoiding* collection calls. You might find yourself in a situation where a bill collector is able to get you on the phone, and in Chapter 5 I will explain how to *discourage* a collector from calling you in the future.

In Part Two, we assume that bill collectors are being professional and obeying the law in their dealings with you. However, at times they may do things that are unprofessional, illegal, or even criminal. Part Five, "How to Deal with Unprofessional Bill Collectors," explains which of a bill collector's behaviours might be considered a criminal offence, as well as the actions you can take in response. Many of these actions will cause the collector to stop calling you.

CHAPTER 3

YOUR LEGAL RIGHT TO STOP OR RESTRICT COLLECTION CALLS

Your ability to stop collection calls will depend on (1) who is calling you, (2) which province you live in, (3) whether these calls are being made to your home, your workplace, or your cellphone, and (4) in some cases, the geographic location the calls are being made from.

If your goal is to stop collection calls, I have a homework assignment for you: first find out who is calling you. Are the calls coming from your creditor, a debt buyer, a collection agency, or a law firm? In addition, where are the calls being placed from? (For more information on how to figure out who is calling you, see Chapter 23, "Going on the Offensive.") This is important because each Canadian province and territory has a law restricting the conduct of collection agencies – for example, the times of day they can call you and the number of calls they can make within a certain period. These laws vary across the country.

IMPORTANT FACT
You do not have a legal obligation to speak to bill collectors. You have every right to decline to speak to them, and if they do get you on the phone you have every right to hang up.

STOPPING CALLS FROM A COLLECTION AGENCY

You might be fortunate enough to live in one of the five provinces or the one territory whose residents have the right to take some action to stop collection calls: Alberta, British Columbia, the Northwest Territories, Nova Scotia, Ontario, and Quebec (see Figure 1). If you do and you exercise your right to stop the calls, it is illegal for a collection agency to call you – period! Thank your lucky stars if you live there. In British Columbia this law also applies to creditors, debt buyers, and employees of law firms, but everywhere else a different set of rules applies. Unfortunately, if you are a resident of Manitoba, New Brunswick, Newfoundland, Nunavut, Prince Edward Island, Saskatchewan, or Yukon you do not have the right to stop collection calls from collection agencies based in Canada, so you might want to skip the next few pages.

Figure 1: Provinces giving residents the right to stop collection calls

	COLLECTION AGENCIES	CREDITORS AND LAW FIRMS
Alberta	•	
British Columbia	•	•
Manitoba		
New Brunswick		
Newfoundland		
Northwest Territories	•	
Nova Scotia	•	
Nunavut		
Ontario	•	
Prince Edward Island		
Quebec	•	
Saskatchewan		
Yukon Territory		

In the next few pages I will cover what a resident of Alberta, British Columbia, the Northwest Territories, Nova Scotia, Ontario, and Quebec has to do in order to stop a collection agency from contacting him. When you successfully exercise the right to stop a collection agency from calling you, it usually cannot communicate directly with you in writing as well.

Alberta

If you are an Alberta resident you can stop future collection calls from a collection agency by advising it

1. that you are not the debtor, in which case the agency is not permitted to call you unless it takes reasonable precautions to confirm that you are, in fact, the debtor;
2. not to call you at work, then making reasonable alternative arrangements to discuss the debt at a mutually convenient time;
3. to communicate directly with your representative, providing the agency with your representative's contact information, and then having your representative make reasonable arrangements to discuss the debt with the collector at a mutually convenient time. (The representative can be a family member, friend, or anyone else you trust; see suggested wording in the following example); or
4. in writing that you dispute owing the debt and that you want your creditor to take you to court.

British Columbia

If you are a resident of British Columbia you can stop future collection calls from a collection agency, *as well as your original creditor, a company that has purchased your debt, and a lawyer or a lawyer's employees,* by advising it in writing

Sample Notice That You Are Represented by an Agent

(your name)
(your street address)
(city, province, postal code)

(date)

WITHOUT PREJUDICE:

(name of collection agency)
(street address)
(city, province, postal code)

Dear Sir/Mme.:

Re: (your name)
     (name of your creditor)
     (your account number)

I am writing you in connection with the above-noted account. I under-stand that your collection agency is attempting to collect this account.

This will confirm that (name of individual) will be acting as my agent in this matter. (Name of individual) is a (lawyer, paralegal, family member, friend, relative, et cetera). Furthermore, I authorize you to discuss the above-noted matter with my agent. The contact information for my agent is as follows:

(name of individual)
(mailing address)
(city, province, postal code)
(telephone number)
(e-mail address)

Since I am represented by an agent in this matter, do not communicate with me directly in any matter whatsoever.

Sincerely,

(your signature)
(your name)

1. that you dispute the debt and you want your creditor to take you to court;
2. that you want it to communicate with your lawyer only, and then providing your lawyer's name and mailing address; or
3. that you want it to communicate with you in writing only, and then providing your mailing address.

Northwest Territories

If you are a resident of the Northwest Territories you can stop a collection agency from making future collection calls by advising it

1. to communicate with you only in writing; or
2. that it is only to communicate with your lawyer, and then providing the collection agency with your lawyer's name, address, and telephone number.

Nova Scotia

If you are a resident of Nova Scotia you can stop a collection agency from making future collection calls by advising it in writing to communicate with your lawyer, and providing your lawyer's name, address, and telephone number.

Ontario

If you are an Ontario resident you can stop future collection calls from a collection agency by advising it

1. that you are not the debtor, in which case the agency is not permitted to call or write to you until it takes all reasonable precautions to confirm that you are, in fact, the debtor;
2. by registered mail, that you dispute owing the debt and you request that the matter go to court; or

3. by registered mail (or have your lawyer do so), that you are represented by a lawyer, and providing the lawyer's contact information in this letter.

If you are an Ontario resident, the most effective way to stop a collection agency from calling you about an account is to have a lawyer send a registered letter to the collection agency advising it that he represents you on that account.

Quebec
If you are a Quebec resident you can stop a collection agency from making future collection calls by advising it

1. that you are not the debtor;
2. to communicate with your lawyer; or
3. in writing, and before legal action is commenced, that you dispute the debt and your creditor may proceed with a legal action.

STOPPING CALLS FROM A LAWYER'S OFFICE
You should be able to stop collection calls from a lawyer's office by hiring your own lawyer to write a letter saying that you are now represented by her. It would then be considered professional misconduct for the first lawyer or any of his staff to make further phone calls to you. This applies to residents of *any* province.

STOPPING COLLECTION CALLS ORIGINATING FROM OUTSIDE CANADA
Under the U.S. Fair Debt Collection Practices Act (FDCPA) you can stop collection calls from a collection agency or a law firm if the calls are being made from within the United States. You will need to write it a "cease and desist" letter that satisfies certain requirements under the FDCPA (see the following sample). If you continue to receive collection calls after you send the cease and

Sample Cease and Desist Letter Sent to U.S. Debt Collector

(your name)
(your street address)
(city, province, postal code)

(date)

                                              SENT BY COURIER:
(name of collection agency or law firm)
(street address)
(city, state, zip code)

Dear Sir/Mme.;

Re: (your name)
   (name of your creditor)
   (your account number)

I am writing you in connection with the above-noted account, which I understand that your firm has been attempting to collect from me.

I am exercising my right under the federal *Fair Debt Collection Practices Act (FDCPA)* to stop you from communicating with me in the future regarding this account. This will confirm that I refuse to pay this account. Furthermore, I do not wish to receive any further communications from your firm regarding this account.

Should you communicate with me in the future, you should anticipate that I will sue your firm seeking damages under the *FDCPA*.

Govern yourself accordingly,

(your signature)
(your name)

desist letter, you will be in a position to sue the collector for monetary damages under the FDCPA.

The other thing you can do if you are receiving collection calls from a collection agency or a law firm situated in the United States, *or from anywhere else outside Canada,* is to contact the organization responsible for licensing and regulating collection agencies in your province (see Appendix C, "Collection Agency Licensing

Administrators"). Odds are the collection agency or law firm does not hold a valid collection agency licence in your province or territory and is therefore contacting you illegally. If that is the case, you can make a written complaint to the licensing administrator in your province indicating that you are receiving collection calls from an unlicensed collection agency.

WHAT TO DO IF THE COLLECTION CALLS CONTINUE

If you exercise your right to stop collection calls, it is illegal for a collection agency to phone you – period! If the collection agency continues to contact you, you have a number of options. First, you can write a letter of complaint to the body responsible for licensing and regulating collection agencies in your province. Second, you can write a letter of complaint to senior management at the collection agency. Third, you can write a letter of complaint to the creditor on whose behalf the collection agency is making these calls. If a Canadian law firm continues to contact you after it receives written notice that you are represented by a lawyer, the collection lawyer is guilty of professional misconduct. You can file a complaint with the law society in the province where the lawyer's office is located. We cover these options in more detail in Chapter 25, "Making an Effective Complaint."

You may also find that you have exercised your right to stop a collection agency from contacting you and then later on you start receiving collection notices and calls from a new agency. Your creditor might have withdrawn your account from the old one and forwarded it to a new one. In this situation you will need to communicate with this new collection agency, and exercise your right to stop collection calls all over again.

CHAPTER 4

TIPS FOR AVOIDING COLLECTION CALLS

Those annoying bill collectors always pick the worst times to call. In most provinces it is legal for a collector to call you early on a Saturday morning, or on weekdays as late as 9 p.m. But let's be honest: is there ever a good time for a collector to call you? This is especially the case if the collector makes comments that humiliate you, or if you get repeated phone calls at your workplace and your co-workers are gossiping about why nasty people at a finance company keep phoning you, or why you're getting repeated messages about "an important legal matter" from an unnamed company.

When you are deciding what to do about a debt, *you are making an important financial decision.* If you are going to make a good financial decision you should avoid doing so when you feel psychologically under siege due to frequent and harassing collection calls. This is why it is so important for you to be able to avoid them. If you are constantly being hounded by collection calls, there is a good chance the quality of your decision-making is going to suffer.

Many consumers pay their debts because of what could best be described as extortion. The collector is conveying a message that you are going to receive collection calls, these calls will not be pleasant, and they will not stop until you pay your bill. At some point you may decide that you want to speak to an agent for your creditor about resolving your account. However, if you do, it should be at a time of *your* choosing – not theirs!

Christopher (not his real name) is one of my clients in Nova Scotia. He owes $25,000 on three credit cards, which are all between 30 and 45 days overdue, so the original creditor is still trying to collect on them. Once these accounts are 90 to 180 days overdue they will be sent to a collection agency, at which time I can write a cease and desist letter advising the agency that I represent Christopher. It will then be illegal for the collection agency to communicate with him directly, verbally or in writing. Unfortunately, because creditors are held to different standards of conduct than collection agencies in every province except British Columbia, there is absolutely nothing I can do in the meantime to stop Christopher's creditors from calling him to demand payment of his debt. However, I have been able to give Christopher some practical tips for avoiding collection calls until I can get involved.

This chapter is for those of you who, like Christopher, are currently unable to exercise the right to stop collection calls as outlined in Chapter 3. Your goal should be to develop a strategy for avoiding unwanted calls until you decide you want to speak to a representative from your creditor about your account. The key is to develop a strategy tailored to your situation so you can avoid as many collection calls as possible, from any type of bill collector, and this might involve some creativity on your part as well as the use of certain technology.

This goal can be attained in one of three ways:

1. Keep your phone numbers confidential.
2. Screen your calls.
3. Avoid disclosing your identity over the telephone.

KEEP YOUR PHONE NUMBERS CONFIDENTIAL

It's impossible for bill collectors to call you if they do not have your current telephone number. If they already do, they might be phoning you at your residence, on your cellphone, or at your workplace. We will deal with each of these potential points of contact.

Ideally, you can make yourself unavailable to a bill collector at your home. A very effective way to do this is to obtain an unlisted phone number. Some of my clients do not want to get an unlisted number because they have had the same number for 40 years, or it's awkward for them to get one because they have moved in with relatives or they have roommates. In this type of situation you might consider using a cellphone only instead of a landline, because unlike with traditional home telephone service, there is no directory of cellphone numbers.

If you do have a cellphone and a bill collector is calling you on it, it is relatively simple and inexpensive to change your number. A few months ago I visited the retailer where I purchased my cellphone, and for less than $50 and in less than ten minutes I was able to change my number.

Some collectors employed by your creditor will call you as many as three, four, or even five times a day at your workplace. This may poison your relationship with your employer, your supervisor, and your co-workers.

IMPORTANT FACT

It is very important that neither you nor anyone else give a bill collector the name of your employer, the phone number or address where you work, or any of your other contact information.

If bill collectors do not have your current phone number, they will definitely try to obtain it, by phoning your family members, relatives, neighbours, and former roommates, landlords, and employers. You should advise them all not to share your contact information, particularly your work phone number or the name of your employer, with anyone. Bill collectors may be very creative in prying this information from them. For example, a collector may call someone you know posing as a police officer, claim that you have been seriously injured in a car accident, and ask for the phone number of your employer or your spouse.

You should not do anything to help a bill collector find your current telephone number. This means you should be careful about what information you post on social networking websites. You should avoid mentioning your name on your voicemail on your land line, on your cellphone and, where appropriate, at work. You should also avoid applying for credit unnecessarily. Sometimes when you're shopping, the store clerk will say that if you apply for a store credit card you will get a rebate on your purchase. But if you complete a credit application and provide a current phone number, some, if not all, of your creditors will have access to the contact information on your credit report.

At some point you may decide to call a collector, and when you do, you should make sure you do not unwittingly disclose any of your phone numbers. Bill collectors will often be able to capture your telephone number unless you do something to hide it.

PRACTICAL TIP

If you do telephone a bill collector, press *67 to block your number before making your call, or call from a payphone or some number other than your home, cellphone, or office.

SCREEN YOUR CALLS

Despite your best efforts to keep your phone numbers confidential, a bill collector might obtain your home, cellphone, or work number. However, you can still avoid a collection call by screening your calls.

The most effective and least expensive way to avoid collection calls, but hardly an ideal solution, is not to answer your telephone during those hours when collection agencies are legally permitted to make collection calls (see Appendix B, "Times When Collection Calls Are Prohibited"). Alternatively, you could have another member of your household answer the phone and act as your gatekeeper. You might be able to have someone screen your calls for you at your workplace as well. Another option is to use a simple answering machine (remember not to include your name on the greeting) that permits you to listen to a message as it is being left. You can then decide whether you wish to take the call.

In addition, it is perfectly legal for you to assume a persona different from your own when you are on the phone. You could answer the phone using a fictitious name or you could assume the identity of an imaginary roommate living in the household. If you get a call from someone you don't know you can simply tell the caller the person she is asking for is not in right now and take a message. If you call the number back outside of regular business hours, the voicemail message might reveal information about the person or company calling you.

You can also take advantage of various services available from your telephone company or cellphone provider to avoid collection calls, including voicemail, call display, anonymous caller blocking, and call screening. These services cost just a few dollars per month and discounts may be available when you subscribe to more than one. For details regarding which are available to you, speak to your local telephone company or cellphone service provider.

Some telephone companies offer "basic" and "advanced" voicemail services, for a monthly fee. Basic voicemail simply records the caller's message, which you cannot hear until after the message is left and you retrieve it. With advanced voicemail, when a caller leaves a message you are able to listen to it while it is being left and you have the option of taking the call. Telus offers this advanced voicemail service, which it calls Message Monitor.

Call Display or caller ID services are also helpful. With Call Display you can choose not to answer any calls when you do not recognize the name or number of the person phoning. If your current telephone does not have a Call Display screen, you can either replace your existing telephone with one that does or purchase a Caller ID box at Walmart, Zellers, or an electronics store like The Source by Circuit City for about $10 or $15.

Depending on where you live, you may also be able to subscribe to a service from your local phone company that will block unknown callers.

Block calls as a Bell customer
Bell Canada and Bell Aliant's Call Privacy service, available to landline customers, blocks calls from people whose phone numbers do not appear on Call Display. The Call Privacy feature is available only to a phone customer who is also a Call Display subscriber. When unknown callers phone a number with the Call Privacy service, they are advised to enter their phone number if they want the call to go through.

If they do enter their phone number, the call is put through and you will be able to see the caller's telephone number on your Call Display screen. You can then decide whether to take the call. After any call, including one from a collection agency, you can arrange to block future calls from that telephone number. The Call Privacy service permits you to block up to 12 telephone numbers at any one time. If the unknown caller does not enter his telephone number, the call is terminated or the caller can leave a message, provided you have voicemail or an answering machine.

A Call Privacy subscriber can provide a three-digit passcode to "private" callers such as friends or family members so they can bypass this feature.

Block calls as a Telus customer
Telus offers two different services for blocking unknown callers to your landline: Anonymous Caller ID and Caller Reveal. These

services are available only to Telus customers who also subscribe to the company's Call Display service.

With the Telus Anonymous Caller ID service, all calls for which no phone number is provided are intercepted. Callers whose names are marked "Private" are asked either to unblock their number or state their name before the call will be put through. Callers whose names are marked "Unknown" are asked to state their name. If the call is put through, the subscriber has the opportunity to either see the caller's telephone number or hear the caller's name before deciding whether to take the call.

With the Caller Reveal service, calls from "Private" or "Unknown" numbers are intercepted. Callers are asked to unblock their phone number or enter another number before their call will be put through. The caller's name and phone number will be displayed on the screen if the call is put through.

Telus also offers its landline customers a Call Screen service that allows subscribers to block specific phone numbers. A subscriber can add the last caller to her Call Screen list. Phone numbers on the Call Screen list will not ring through and the screened caller will not be able to leave a message.

AVOID DISCLOSING YOUR IDENTITY OVER THE TELEPHONE

It is illegal for bill collectors to disclose the existence of your debt to anyone other than you or someone else legally responsible for the debt. This is called a *third party disclosure*. When collection agency employees make a third party disclosure, they are likely in violation of the provincial law licensing the collection agency and possibly a provincial privacy law or the federal privacy law known as the Personal Information Protection and Electronic Documents Act (PIPEDA). You can take advantage of this third party disclosure rule to avoid speaking to a collector.

You and the members of your household are *not* legally obligated to provide *any* information to anyone who calls you.

Because of the law prohibiting third party disclosure, a bill collector cannot begin to discuss your outstanding account with you until he can first confirm that you are, in fact, the debtor. Therefore, you can avoid a collection call, even when a bill collector gets you on the phone, if you do not disclose your identity. You and the members of your household can speak on the phone in such a manner that you do not disclose any personal information, especially any about you. Ideally, your household members should not disclose any information to callers whom they do not recognize. The following example illustrates how a household member can assist in avoiding a collection call.

> Household member: Hello.
> Collector: May I speak to John Smith?
> Household member: May I ask who is calling and the purpose of your call?
> Collector: My name is Bill Green. I am calling about an important matter that I need to discuss with John Smith. Is John Smith in?
> Household member: What company are you calling from?
> Collector: I am only permitted to disclose that information to John Smith. Is there a John Smith who lives at this address?
> Household member: I'm sorry. I don't speak with strangers who refuse to identify what company they are calling from. (Hang up the phone.)

If a collector employed by a collection agency gets you on the phone under false pretences – for example, by misrepresenting the name of his employer or the purpose of the call – you have every right to end the call at once. Furthermore, the collector may have violated provincial law against making a false or misleading statement. If this happens, I would suggest that you make a written complaint to the provincial regulator, the creditor on whose behalf the collector is calling, and senior management at the collection agency. We'll get more into that in Part Five, "How to Deal with Unprofessional Bill Collectors."

CHAPTER 5

HOW TO DISCOURAGE A BILL COLLECTOR FROM CALLING YOU

In Chapter 3 we dealt with your right to *stop* collection calls. In Chapter 4 we reviewed practical tips for *avoiding* collection calls. Despite your best efforts to stop or avoid collection calls, a bill collector might get you on the phone and start discussing your account with you. In this chapter I will provide you with ten useful tips for *discouraging* a bill collector from making future collection calls to you.

1. INFORM THE COLLECTOR THAT YOU ARE NOT THE DEBTOR

If you inform a bill collector that she has the wrong person, she should stop calling you, at least temporarily. Most provinces have a law that requires a collection agency to stop calling an individual after the person advises the collection agency that he is not the debtor. In these circumstances, the collection agency is supposed to contact the creditor on whose behalf the calls are being made and confirm that the person is, in fact, the debtor — in which case it can resume collection calls to that person.

Collection agencies are usually not interested in trying to collect an account from the wrong person, but unfortunately, sometimes you might be dealing with a bill collector who is lazy or not very bright. Few people are interested in paying the debts of others. However, some people – senior citizens, new Canadians, or un-sophisticated individuals – might be confused or intimidated into making a payment to a collection agency despite the fact that they do not owe the money. In fairness to collectors, they have heard people say "You've got the wrong person" more than a few times from people who were, in fact, the debtor.

IMPORTANT FACT

In most provinces, it is illegal for a collection agency to make collection calls to you after you have advised the collection agency you are not the debtor *when, in fact, you are not the debtor.*

If you are not the debtor and you advise the collection agency of this fact but the collection calls continue, you should make a written complaint to the provincial regulator, the creditor on whose behalf the collector is calling, or senior management at the collection agency (see Part Five, "How to Deal with Unprofessional Bill Collectors").

2. REQUEST PROOF THAT THE DEBT IS OWING

A very effective strategy for discouraging a collector from making future collection calls to you is to request written proof that you owe the debt. Your creditor may not be able to supply written documentation proving that you owe any money to it. This is especially the case where your overdue account has been sold to a debt buyer, and in some instances the collection agency may stop all further collection activity on your file in response to your request for documentation.

3. ADVISE THE COLLECTOR THAT YOU DISPUTE OWING THE DEBT

You will discourage a collector from making future collection calls to you by saying that you dispute owing the debt. Furthermore, you can inform the collector that you want the opportunity to tell your story to a judge and you hope your creditor is going to sue you. The collector knows that if you sincerely believe you do not owe the debt, even if you do not have a good reason for this belief, the odds of your making a voluntary payment are slim to none.

4. REFUSE TO DISCUSS YOUR ACCOUNT WITH A COLLECTOR

If your account is being worked by one individual collector, you can discourage her from calling you by refusing to discuss your account with her. Your refusal may take a variety of forms. First, you could simply hang up when the collector gets you on the phone. Second, you could tell the collector that you are already dealing directly with your creditor. Finally, you could advise the collector that you will arrange to have your agent or lawyer contact her or the creditor directly.

And remember: you are under no legal obligation to speak to a bill collector who is attempting to collect an account from you.

5. GIVE THE COLLECTOR WRITTEN AUTHORIZATION TO DEAL WITH AN AGENT

You may be able to discourage a collector from contacting you if you fax or mail it a signed letter authorizing it to deal with your representative (see the "Sample Notice That You Are Represented by an Agent" in Chapter 3). In many cases, when a collection agency receives this letter it will have the option of communicating with you or your agent. There are also a number of situations in which a collection agency might be legally obligated to deal with your agent.

6. ADVISE THE COLLECTOR THAT YOUR CONVERSATION IS BEING RECORDED

Advising a collector that your conversation is being recorded will discourage him from making future collection calls. A collector working a desk likely has 200 to 300 other accounts to work this month. Why should he continue calling you and risk generating a complaint that might cost his job? At a minimum, advising a collector that you are recording your conversation should encourage him to act civilized toward you.

Is it illegal to inform a collector that you are recording the conversation when you are not? No. Is it "wrong" for you to tell a collector that you are recording your conversation when you are not? Let me ask you this: is it wrong for creditors, collection agencies, and collection lawyers in Canada to routinely threaten to sue people when they have no intention whatsoever of doing so?

7. INTERROGATE THE COLLECTOR

If you want to discourage *a collector from a collection agency* from calling you again, you might want to interrogate her. At the beginning of the call, you can insist on having her spell her first and last name and providing you with the name of her employer, her employer's complete mailing address, and the name of the creditor on whose behalf she is calling. In most provinces you are legally entitled to receive this information. You could also ask the collector to confirm that the agency she works for is licensed as a collection agency in the province or territory in which you live. If you want to have some fun, ask the collector for her collector licence number. If you ask these questions, she will likely think you are making some kind of complaint against her and be reluctant to call you again.

If you want to discourage a *collector from your creditor* from calling you, ask him to provide you with the spelling of his first and last name. Many collectors employed by creditors will give you only a first name. Who knows if it is really their first name or their stage name, but a real professional would provide you with his *real* first and last name. Why won't some collectors give out their real first and last name? Maybe because their conduct is so outrageous they don't want anyone to be able to identify them, or because their employer does not want them to be identifiable if a consumer records a telephone conversation with them.

8. DEMONSTRATE THAT YOU KNOW MORE THAN THE COLLECTOR DOES

If you want to discourage a collector from calling you, try showing that you know more about the law regulating collection agencies in your province or territory than she does. Each province and territory in Canada has a law regulating the conduct of collectors employed by a collection agency. The specific rules of prohibited conduct are set out in either this law or regulations enacted under this law. For more information, see Chapter 22, "Identifying Bill Collector Misconduct."

Have some fun and let the collector know you are going to be her worst nightmare if she treats you badly. You might even make reference to specific chapters, pages, or information in this book. You have paid money to purchase it. Get your money's worth.

9. ADVISE THE COLLECTOR THAT YOU ARE UNEMPLOYED OR ON SOCIAL ASSISTANCE

As a general rule, you should not disclose any information to a collector, but if you are currently unemployed or supporting yourself on social assistance, you might inform him of this fact. It suggests that you might not be able to pay your outstanding account, unless you can borrow the money from friends or family or sell some of your assets. However, under no circumstances should you discuss your employment prospects or your future career plans with a collector.

10. ADVISE THE COLLECTOR THAT YOU ARE GOING FOR CREDIT COUNSELLING OR WILL BE MEETING WITH A BANKRUPTCY TRUSTEE

You will likely discourage a collector from calling you if you advise him that you intend to go for credit counselling or you will be seeing a bankruptcy trustee. Upon hearing this, a competent collector will ask you at some point for the name of your credit counselling agency or your bankruptcy trustee, so he can call and confirm.

PART THREE

HOW TO AVOID PAYING YOUR OUTSTANDING ACCOUNTS

You may find it hard to believe, but there are a host of reasons that you might never have to pay an outstanding unsecured consumer debt. This fact might help explain why large creditors are often prepared to settle accounts for significantly less than 100 cents on the dollar once an account is a few months in default, and at progressively greater discounts as time goes on. There are five reasons, some *legal* and some *practical,* that you might never have to pay an outstanding account:

1. The limitation period on your debt has expired (Chapter 6).
2. Your creditor might not be able to prove your debt is owing (Chapter 7).
3. You might never be sued on your account (Chapter 8).
4. Your creditor will be unable to enforce a judgment against you (Chapter 9).
5. You might be able to sue your creditor or the bill collector.

In this section I devote an entire chapter to each of the first four reasons. The fifth one is a bit more complicated. You might be able to avoid paying a delinquent account, in whole or in part, because you have some kind of legal claim against your creditor or your creditor's collection agent. For instance, you may have taken your car in to get your brakes fixed at Acme Garage, and you were charged $1,000 for the job. You and your family then went on vacation, your brakes did not work properly, and you ended up paying another garage $900 to have your brakes fixed. In this example, you would have a $900 claim against Acme Garage. You could also have a legal claim because of misconduct by the collection agency or one of its employees. If you do have a legal claim involving a significant amount of money, your creditor is much less likely to sue you or aggressively pursue money from you because this would be tantamount to running inside a burning building. For more information on commencing a lawsuit, see Chapter 26, "Suing a Bill Collector."

In Chapter 10, I give tips for reducing the odds that your creditor, or in some cases, a collection agency, will sue you. Finally, in Chapter 11, I will explain the consequences of failing to pay your account.

IMPORTANT FACT

If you contact the offices of a credit counselling agency or a bankruptcy trustee, you should not expect them to give you any information whatsoever about the reasons you might not have to pay an account. Before you contact either of them, you should read Part Three in its entirety.

CHAPTER 6

THE LIMITATION PERIOD ON YOUR DEBT HAS EXPIRED

You might be able to avoid paying an unsecured debt because of the passage of time and the expiry of what is called a *limitation period*. Limitation periods may be your best friend if you have debts. There is a good chance you will never hear this term if you are speaking to a credit counsellor or a bankruptcy trustee. In my experience, the only group of people in Canada who seem to know much about limitation periods are lawyers.

Limitation periods are typically found in a provincial law called a statute of limitations, except in Quebec, where it is in the Civil Code of Quebec. A statute of limitations is a law that forces creditors to sue debtors within a specified number of years. Your creditor will effectively lose the ability to collect a debt from you after the limitation period expires, unless (1) your creditor sues you and you fail to file an appropriate defence with the court or (2) you choose to pay the debt voluntarily. Please note that consumers can normally take advantage of the statute of limitations only on unsecured consumer debt. This means that the expiry of a limitation period is likely of no value to you if your debt is owed to the government or it is secured debt.

Every week thousands of Canadians make payments to collection agencies, in circumstances where a limitation period has expired, when in fact they could have declined to pay the debt *without any adverse financial consequences* except possibly a negative impact on their credit score. When I did collection work, my law firm would collect thousands of dollars from consumers like you on behalf of chartered banks and on accounts that were as much as 13 years old. People paid accounts even though they didn't have to. Maybe they just didn't know better. Or maybe some of them were motivated to repay the account because morally it seemed like the right thing to do. Unfortunately for those people, there is a good chance their original creditor never received their payment because the account may have been sold to a debt buyer by that point.

IMPORTANT FACT

Regardless of where you live in Canada, if you have an unsecured consumer account for which (1) you have not made a payment in the last six years and (2) you have not made a written acknowledgement of the debt during the past six years, you are in a position to avoid paying this account with no adverse consequences to your credit score.

The statute of limitations begins to run on the date of your default (the date of your last payment on a specific account), or the date of your last written acknowledgement of your indebtedness, whichever occurs later. In most instances, the limitation period begins to run on the date of your last payment. Here's an example of how this works:

One of my clients, Jim, a Manitoba resident, stopped making payments on his ABC Mart credit card on January 30, 2004. The statute of limitations in Manitoba is six years. Therefore, the limitation period on Jim's debt would have expired on January 30, 2010, six years after the date of his last payment. Unfortunately, Jim wrote a letter dated June

1, 2008, to ABC *Mart, in which he acknowledged owing money to* ABC *Mart even though at that point he was on disability and was not in a financial position to pay the account. This letter constituted Jim's written acknowledgement of the debt, thereby restarting the six-year clock on the Manitoba statute of limitations. Instead of this debt expiring on January 30, 2010, it will now expire on June 1, 2014 (six years after Jim's written acknowledgement of the debt), unless Jim does something you might consider foolish, like make a partial payment or make another written acknowledgement of the debt – which would extend the limitation period an additional six years.*

IMPORTANT FACT

There are two things you can do *before the limitation period expires* on your debt to restart the clock on the statute of limitations: make a partial payment or make a written acknowledgement of the debt.

Figure 2 summarizes Canadian limitation periods that are relevant in the context of debt collection.

Figure 2: Limitation periods in Canada

PROVINCE OR TERRITORY	LIMITATION PERIOD FOR CONSUMER DEBTS
Alberta	2 years
British Columbia	6 years
Manitoba	6 years
New Brunswick	6 years
Newfoundland & Labrador	6 years
Northwest Territories	6 years
Nova Scotia	6 years
Nunavut	6 years
Ontario	2 years*
Prince Edward Island	6 years
Quebec	3 years

| Saskatchewan | 2 years |
| Yukon Territory | 6 years |

* The limitation period in Ontario is 2 years for claims arising after January 1, 2004, and 6 years for claims arising before January 1, 2004.

IMPORTANT FACT

If you want to rely upon the expiry of a limitation period to avoid paying a debt, it is very important that you have a good grasp of how limitation periods work.

The expiry of a limitation period has different consequences depending upon which province you live in. If you live in British Columbia or Newfoundland and Labrador, on the date the limitation period expires, your debt is *extinguished* and the debt no longer exists. It is then illegal for your creditor or its collection agent to attempt to collect the account from you.

If you live anywhere else in Canada, the expiry of a limitation period does not extinguish a debt, it only provides you with an *affirmative defence* that can be raised if you are sued. In other words, if your creditor sues you after the expiry of a limitation period and you file a defence with the court citing the expiry of a limitation period as a defence, your creditor will not be able to successfully sue you. However, if your creditor sues you after the expiry of a limitation period and you *fail* to file the defence, your creditor will likely be able to successfully obtain a judgment against you. We will learn more about the mechanics of lawsuits in Chapters 9 and 10.

Therefore, unless you live in British Columbia or Newfoundland, it is perfectly legal for your creditor or its authorized collection agent to send you collection notices and make collection calls after the expiry of a limitation period. However, under Alberta law, it is illegal for a collection agency to attempt to collect a debt from you six years after the date of your last payment, unless your creditor has successfully sued you and obtained a judgment against you.

IMPORTANT FACT

Failure to pay an outstanding account may result in a negative impact on your credit rating.

Under provincial law and the internal policies at Equifax and TransUnion, your outstanding consumer debt is supposed to be removed from your credit report six years from the date of last activity, usually the date of your last payment.

LIMITATION PERIODS AND DEBTS OWING TO GOVERNMENTS

Up to this point this chapter has dealt with limitation periods and their impact on consumer debt, which does not include a debt owing to the government. The statute of limitations in four provinces – Alberta, Saskatchewan, Ontario, and Newfoundland – says that the provincial government is bound by the Act. In the rest of Canada the provincial or territorial governments are not bound by the statute of limitations, which means a consumer cannot take advantage of it if they owe money to the provincial government.

Ontario residents cannot rely on the expiry of a limitation period if the government is collecting fines, taxes, penalties, and interest, or the money owing is in connection with student loans, awards and grants, and social assistance payments. Newfoundland residents cannot take advantage of a limitation period if the provincial government is seeking to recover a fine or other penalty. In Saskatchewan a resident cannot take advantage of a limitation period if the provincial government is collecting an unpaid fine.

IMPORTANT FACT

A resident of Alberta, Saskatchewan, or Newfoundland and Labrador might be able to successfully rely on the expiry of a limitation period to avoid paying a provincial student loan.

USING THE EXPIRY OF A LIMITATION PERIOD AS A DEFENCE AT SOME FUTURE DATE

You might find yourself in the position today where you cannot take advantage of the expiry of a limitation period to avoid paying a debt. However, this does not mean that you cannot take advantage of a limitation period.

IMPORTANT FACT

You would be in a position to avoid paying an unsecured consumer debt at some future date if you cease making payments on your debt, provided your creditor does not commence a lawsuit against you before the expiry of the relevant limitation period.

I refer to this as the *wait-it-out strategy.* Thousands of Canadians would have been better off employing the wait-it-out strategy instead of enrolling in credit counselling, making a consumer proposal, or filing for personal bankruptcy. This is particularly the case in provinces where limitation periods are short: three years in Quebec, and only two in Alberta, Saskatchewan, and Ontario.

Furthermore, as you will learn in Part Four of this book, once you stop making payments on an outstanding account – and unless you are sued – you will be in a position to negotiate a generous lump sum settlement of less than 100 cents on the dollar with your creditor and its collection agent as your debt ages. Even if you are sued, it will likely be possible for you to negotiate some kind of settlement because otherwise your creditor may have to wait years to recover its money. Even in the worst case scenario, if you are sued on one or more of your outstanding accounts you will still have a number of options available to you, including debt settlement, credit counselling, making a consumer proposal, or filing for personal bankruptcy.

CHAPTER 7

YOUR CREDITOR MIGHT NOT BE ABLE TO PROVE YOUR DEBT IS OWING

If a creditor can't prove that you owe a debt, you cannot be held legally responsible for it. So you might want to insist that a bill collector provide you with documentation proving that you owe money to your creditor. It puts the collector on the defensive and may discourage her from calling you. After all, why is she bothering you and demanding money from you when she can't even prove you owe it in the first place? Your request for documentation might also motivate the collector to cease all activity on your account. Some creditors even instruct their collectors to cease work on a file as soon as a consumer requests supporting documentation, especially if the balance is relatively small or it is owned by a debt buyer.

PRACTICAL TIP
If the collector doesn't already have your home address or workplace address, try to obtain proof that you owe the bill without disclosing that information – for example, by having it faxed to a local postal outlet or mailed to a friend's address.

A collection agency will almost never possess any paperwork proving you owe money to a creditor, but it will often follow up with the creditor to get the proof. Creditors don't generally like these requests, because digging it up takes too much time, trouble, and expense. In fact, some creditors outright refuse to provide collection agencies with supporting documentation. I used to manage the legal department at a number of collection agencies, and it never ceased to amaze me how uncooperative some creditors were on this front.

If the collector does come up with supporting documents, it's possible they will reveal that the collection agency was demanding an incorrect amount of money from you. The creditor might have provided the collection agency with incorrect information at the very beginning, through a simple data entry error. They could even have the wrong person altogether. Maybe your son, who has the same name as you, and who lived at home with you for a while, owes the money.

HOW THIS CAN HELP YOU IN A LAWSUIT

If you are receiving collection calls for an unsecured debt that you legitimately owe, your creditor may sue you to recover the money. However, to succeed with its lawsuit, the creditor must be able to prove that you do owe the debt. The *burden of proof* is on your creditor.

When a creditor sues, it hopes that one of two things will happen: either you will agree to settle your account for a lump sum payment in the immediate future, usually within 15 to 30 days, or you will fail to file a defence, enabling your creditor to obtain a judgment against you without the time, trouble, and expense of having a trial. A *judgment* is an order of the court in favour of your creditor against you. A judgment is for a specific dollar amount and it may include interest.

IMPORTANT FACT

If you've been sued you might want to discuss your situation with a lawyer or a competent paralegal. Some provinces have a Lawyer Referral Program under which you can receive 20 to 30 minutes of free advice from a lawyer over the telephone. If you've been sued in small claims court, you might want to speak to a counter person at your local small claims court.

If you do defend a lawsuit, your creditor might still obtain a judgment against you after the case goes to trial. However, if you do *not* file a defence to your creditor's lawsuit in a timely fashion, your creditor will be entitled to obtain what is referred to as a *default judgment.*

IMPORTANT FACT

If you are sued on a debt, there is a real possibility that your creditor cannot produce documents at trial that would enable it to win the lawsuit, particularly if the creditor is a large financial institution. So even if you legitimately owe a debt, you may want to consider defending a lawsuit brought by your creditor.

The burden of proof that your creditor must satisfy to obtain a judgment against you is much lower if you do not file a defence, and the creditor might be able to obtain one even if it lacks proof that you owe it any money. When I did collection work, I successfully sued a dozen consumers on behalf of one of Canada's largest banks when the consumers had defaulted on their credit cards or personal loans. The bank was unable to provide any documentation whatsoever to prove that these people owed it any money. Ideally, the bank would have provided me with a photocopy of the consumers' signed credit card or loan applications and copies of their monthly credit card statements. The bank gave me absolutely nothing!

I simply made a photocopy of the notelines on the collection agency's software containing the creditor's name, the consumer's name and mailing address, the consumer's account number, and the balance owing. I attached this photocopy to the *Plaintiff's Claim,* the form used to commence a lawsuit in Ontario Small Claims Court. If one of these consumers had filed a defence with the court, I would have had to abandon the lawsuit before it went to trial, because it would not have been possible to satisfy the burden of proof that the consumer owed the bank any money.

Have you ever been in a government office and they had problems finding your file? I sure have. In many ways large financial institutions are no different from the government: they are bureaucracies and they too often destroy, lose, or misfile documents. If you are sued by a large financial institution, it might not be able to produce documents proving that you owe money to it.

Your creditor is either going to be able to produce documents proving that you owe money or it is not. Even if it can produce proof, it is not the end of the world. Depending on your situation, you might be able to settle the lawsuit for a lump sum payment worth less than the full amount your creditor sued you for. Even if you abandon your defence of the lawsuit, the worst thing that could happen is that your creditor obtains a judgment against you and then attempts to obtain a garnishment order against your bank accounts or your wages. Under a *wage garnishment order,* some or all of your wages might be exempt from garnishment. We will learn more about what happens when a creditor successfully sues an individual in Chapter 9, "Your Creditor Will Be Unable to Enforce a Judgment Against You."

YOU MIGHT NEVER BE SUED ON YOUR OUTSTANDING ACCOUNT

If you are unable or unwilling to pay your outstanding account, your creditor will typically be able to recover money from you only by suing you – unless things change and you voluntarily pay up.

There are only two exceptions to this general rule. As noted earlier, if you owe money to a financial institution where you also have assets, the financial institution may exercise a *right of set-off* to recover the money. For example, if you default on your ABC Bank credit card payments and you have a savings account at ABC Bank, once you deposit money in that account, the bank could seize it to pay off money owing on the credit card. Similarly, the federal government routinely "claws back" income tax refunds and GST rebates from individuals owing money to it, or it freezes their bank accounts.

A large creditor such as a bank, credit card company, retailer, or utility will probably decide whether to sue you within the first six months of your defaulting on your payments. As we will see in the next chapter, even if your creditor wins a lawsuit against you, there is no guarantee that it will recover any money from you, so creditors are very cautious about suing consumers. A creditor that is undisciplined and reckless can actually lose thousands of dollars suing a single file and never recover any money owing.

Instead of suing, creditors often prefer to send an outstanding account to a collection agency – so if your account has been sent to a collection agency, the odds of your being sued are low. In fact, I estimate that all of the collection agencies in Canada put together sue fewer than one in 10,000 consumer accounts. You should remember that the next time a collector from a collection agency gets you on the phone and threatens to sue you if you do not pay your account in full by Friday.

So your creditor might *never* sue you on your unsecured consumer debt, typically money owing on a credit card, personal loan, line of credit, bank overdraft or to a utility, such as a phone company, cellphone provider, or Internet or cable television provider. (This doesn't include debts owed to the federal government.)

If you owe money on a consumer debt and your creditor is never going to sue you, all you have to do is to wait for the limitation period to expire and then you have a good defence. You can avoid paying your outstanding account altogether! Of course, this will have a negative impact on your credit rating for six years from the date of your last payment.

If your creditor is never going to sue you, you are also in an excellent position to negotiate a very generous lump sum settlement with your creditor – and the longer you wait, the less you'll likely have to pay to settle it. Most major creditors – banks, credit card issuers, major retailers, and utilities – will negotiate a lump sum settlement for 20 cents to 35 cents on the dollar, and sometimes less, when an account is 36 months in default. In 2009 I routinely settled debts owing to one particular creditor on behalf of my clients for lump sum payments as low as 12 cents to 20 cents on the dollar, and the accounts had been in default for only six or seven months. In other words, if a client owed $30,000, the creditor called it even when they paid as little as $3,600. When you settle an account, your credit report should be updated by your creditor, or its collection agent, within 60 days, to show that the account has been settled in full and that you have a zero balance owing.

WHEN A CREDITOR IS MOST LIKELY TO SUE

For a creditor to sue a consumer, it must be able to answer yes to the following questions:

1. Can we find the consumer?
2. Can we commence a lawsuit before the expiry of the limitation period?
3. Does the consumer owe more than $5,000 or $10,000, in which case it might be worthwhile suing?
4. Does the consumer have the capacity to pay the debt – sufficient assets, income, or the ability to borrow money?

Your creditor will not usually consider suing you unless it can answer yes to each of those questions. In some cases, a creditor that had no intention of suing you might change its mind because at some point you provided it or its collection agent with certain information: your current address, information about any property you own, details about your employment, or banking information.

When I was managing a collection agency's legal department, one key piece of information I wanted to know was whether a consumer disputed owing an account. If he did not dispute it, I was more inclined to sue, because the odds were much higher that we could win a default judgment, which meant avoiding the time, trouble, and expense of having a trial.

IMPORTANT FACT

You should never disclose any personal information to your creditor or its collection agent, such as your address or place of work. Nothing you can say will discourage them from suing you except that you support yourself on social assistance or you are currently unemployed.

There are certain kinds of people creditors are more likely to sue. Your creditor might be interested in suing you if you fall into one of the following categories:

1. You own real property in your own name and you have significant equity in the property to satisfy a debt.
2. You have a good job with a good income, your wages are not currently subject to a garnishment order, and you have no outstanding court judgments.
3. You have a unionized job, you make more than $25,000 a year, your wages are not currently subject to a garnishment order, and you have no outstanding judgments.

If you own real property in your own name, a creditor will be motivated to sue you and then put a lien on your home, townhouse, condominium, farm, cottage, or rental property. Depending on your situation, your creditor might be interested in suing you and then pursuing a wage garnishment. We will learn more about this topic in the next chapter.

EIGHT REASONS THAT YOUR CREDITOR MIGHT NEVER SUE YOU

Even if you owe money to your creditor, there are eight reasons that you might never be sued on your outstanding account. Almost all of the reasons involve practical considerations rather than legal ones.

IMPORTANT FACT
Credit counsellors and bankruptcy trustees are unlikely to provide you with any information about the eight reasons that you might never be sued on an outstanding account.

1. Your creditor cannot locate you

Your creditor will have difficulty successfully recovering money from you if it cannot find you. For your creditor to sue you, it typically has to serve a legal document on you to commence the lawsuit. Service of this court document is done either by personally handing the document to the debtor, handing the document to an adult at the debtor's residence, or mailing the document to the debtor's residence.

2. Your creditor has no information about how it can satisfy a judgment against you

Even if your creditor knows your current address, it will be reluctant to sue you unless it can confirm that you have the capacity to satisfy a judgment. In other words, your creditor will likely not sue you unless it can confirm that you own real property in your name and that you have some equity in the property, or that it can successfully do a wage garnishment or identify your bank branch in order to seize money in your bank account.

3. The limitation period on your account has expired

Your creditor will be reluctant to sue you if the limitation period on your unsecured consumer debt has expired. However, it is possible for your creditor to sue you, obtain a judgment against you, and recover money from you if you have not filed a defence relying upon the expiry of the limitation period. If you inform your creditor or its collection agent that you do not dispute owing an account, your creditor might be tempted to sue you in the hopes of getting a default judgment. If you file a defence, your creditor could always abandon the lawsuit.

4. You owe less than $10,000

Even if you owe more than $10,000 on an outstanding account, you may never be sued. However, all things being equal, your creditor will be more motivated to sue you if you owe $12,000 than if you owe $3,000. Suing you involves a significant amount of time, trouble, and expense for your creditor. In many cases it is simply more cost-effective to send your account to a collection agency.

As a general rule, if you owe less than $5,000 to a large creditor, the odds are very low that you will be sued. If you owe between $5,000 and $10,000 to a major creditor there is a good chance that you will never be sued. On the other hand, if you owe $4,500 to your dentist, there is a significant chance that your dentist is going to sue you in small claims court.

Jane, an Ontario resident, owes $60,000 in unsecured debt, on credit cards, personal loans, and utilities such as her cellphone, Internet, and cable service. Her debts are as follows:

Credit cards
Bank One	$4,000
Bank Two	$4,000
Bank Three	$4,000
Bank Four	$4,000
Retailer One	$4,000
Retailer Two	$4,000
Retailer Three	$4,000
Retailer Four	$4,000
Retailer Five	$4,000
Retailer Six	$4,000

Personal loans
Bank One	$4,000
Bank Two	$4,000
Bank Three	$4,000

Lines of credit
Bank One	$4,000

Utilities
Cellphone	$4,000
Total Debt	*$60,000*

Jane owns a home and has a good job. She is not sure what to do. She has not made a payment on any of these debts in three months. Should she get a debt consolidation loan, go for credit counselling, or speak to a bankruptcy trustee about making a consumer proposal or filing for personal bankruptcy? Since Jane owes less than $5,000 to each creditor, there is a good chance she will not be sued on any of these accounts.

Jane might be best off choosing not to make any payments on some or all of these accounts. She can wait 21 more months for the expiry of Ontario's two-year limitation period, after which she will have avoided paying $60,000 in debt – although this will have a negative impact on her credit rating. Instead, over the next few years, Jane could settle these outstanding accounts by negotiating lump sum settlements with her creditors at major savings. Using this strategy Jane could probably eliminate this $60,000 in debt for approximately $15,000 to $20,000, or 25 per cent to 30 per cent of the amount currently owing.

5. You support yourself on social assistance or you are unemployed

If you support yourself on social assistance the odds are very low that your creditor will sue you. In many provinces, the law prohibits creditors from seizing social assistance payments from consumers. If you are supporting yourself on social assistance, it is most likely illegal for a creditor who has successfully sued you to seize money from your bank account. However, some creditors or their collection agents still try to do this.

6. You have a low-paying job you could quit tomorrow

Most people who have a job that pays the minimum wage and whose wages become subject to a garnishment order will quit their job and get a new one to avoid having money deducted from their paycheque. Creditors know this and, therefore, they are reluctant to sue people who have low-paying jobs.

7. Your creditor might be concerned about the negative publicity or a potential counterclaim if it were to sue you

In some situations your creditor might choose not to sue you because of the potential bad publicity that might arise if it were to do so. For example, a Canadian chartered bank might be reluctant to sue an 85-year-old widow if she co-signed a loan for her husband and the only way the bank could satisfy its judgment was to put a lien on her home – which would effectively put the widow out on the street.

Your creditor might also be reluctant to sue you if the conduct of the creditor's employees or its collection agent has been reprehensible or offensive to the general public. In that case they fear both bad publicity and the possibility of your filing a counterclaim seeking financial compensation. This is especially true if you are dealing with a major financial institution such as a bank that spends millions of dollars promoting its image.

8. You live in New Brunswick and you rent

The odds of your being sued in New Brunswick are low unless you own a home, townhouse, condominium, farm, cottage, or rental property in your own name and you have significant equity in the property. New Brunswick is the only province in Canada that does not give a creditor with a judgment against a debtor the right to seize money in a bank account or a portion of a debtor's wages under a garnishment order. I remember discussing this issue with a senior civil servant responsible for licensing collection agencies in New Brunswick, back when I was doing collection work, and she described the province as "a debtor's haven."

CHAPTER 9

YOUR CREDITOR WILL BE UNABLE TO ENFORCE A JUDGMENT AGAINST YOU

You may legitimately owe an unsecured debt, and then your creditor sues you and obtains a judgment against you. Things still aren't as bad as they might seem. Even if you do have the money to pay a creditor, you are under no legal obligation to voluntarily pay it to satisfy an outstanding judgment. You do not, for example, have to borrow cash from your family or sell some of your assets in order to give the creditor a cheque. The onus is on your creditor to take some action to attempt to recover money from you owing on a judgment.

The fact that your creditor has obtained a judgment against you (you're now known as a *judgment debtor*) simply means that your creditor, now known as a *judgment creditor,* has some tools at its disposal known as *enforcement remedies* to assist it in recovering money you owe it.

IMPORTANT FACT

The fact that your creditor has obtained a judgment against you is no guarantee that your creditor is ever going to recover some or all of the money you owe it.

ENFORCEMENT REMEDIES AVAILABLE TO JUDGMENT CREDITORS IN CANADA

The enforcement remedies most commonly used by judgment creditors are wage garnishments, garnishment of a bank account, and placing a lien or *writ of execution* on real property (or real estate) that is held in your own name, including your home, townhouse, condominium, cottage, farm, or rental property. This most commonly happens with a debtor's principal residence when his name is on the property title.

IMPORTANT FACT

The enforcement remedies available to a judgment creditor in your province are determined by provincial law and are not uniform across Canada.

Under a *garnishment order* a court orders someone owing you money to pay some of that money into court. The court in turn forwards this money to your creditor. It is common for a creditor who successfully sues you to obtain a wage garnishment, except in New Brunswick, where this option is unavailable. Similarly, if you are a New Brunswick resident your judgment creditor cannot seize money from your bank account under a garnishment order.

Everywhere else in Canada, your creditor has the right to serve a garnishment order on anyone who owes you money, including the following:

- Your employer, if you are a salaried employee
- Your broker, if you are a real estate agent who works on commission
- One of your clients, if you are self-employed
- Your tenant, if you rent out a suite in your home
- Your bank branch, to seize money in your bank account
- A party to a lawsuit that owes you money (e.g., the defendant in a lawsuit involving a motor vehicle accident)

- The estate of a deceased person in circumstances where you will inherit money

This chapter will explain the details of each enforcement remedy.

Wage garnishment

Your creditor will likely not be interested in suing you and obtaining a wage garnishment in any one of the following four scenarios:

1. You earn less than $20,000 a year *with a single employer.*
2. A significant portion of the compensation you receive is in the form of cash, such as tips that a server would earn working at a restaurant.
3. You have a job you would quit tomorrow if your wages were subject to a garnishment order.
4. You live in New Brunswick.

If your creditor successfully sues you, it can file the necessary paperwork with the court in order to obtain a wage garnishment, which is served on your employer. This is an order requiring your employer to pay a portion of your wages to the court, instead of to you. The money is then forwarded by the court to your creditor to satisfy your creditor's judgment. A wage garnishment will end under a variety of circumstances: when your judgment is satisfied, if your creditor agrees to terminate the garnishment as part of a settlement, or you stop working for your employer.

If you learn about a wage garnishment order, there are several things you can do to end it:

1. You can quit your job.
2. You can negotiate a settlement with your creditor.
3. You can make a consumer proposal or file for personal bankruptcy.

At the end of this chapter you will learn more about how it might be possible to reduce the amount of money you would otherwise pay under a wage garnishment order.

Under provincial law, some of an employee's wages are *exempt* from a wage garnishment. The size of this exemption varies from province to province (see Figure 3). In Ontario, for example, 80 per cent of an employee's take-home pay is exempt from garnishment under the Ontario Wages Act. In contrast, in British Columbia and Manitoba, only 70 per cent of an employee's take-home pay is exempt from a wage garnishment. For more information on the exemptions available in the province in which you live, please visit my website, www.helpwithcollectioncalls.ca.

Figure 3: Provincial exemptions from wage garnishments

PROVINCE OR TERRITORY	EXEMPTION FROM WAGE GARNISHMENT
Alberta	The maximum monthly exemption is $2,400, plus $200 per dependant, and the minimum monthly exemption is $800, plus $200 per dependant.
British Columbia	70 per cent of your take-home pay is exempt from wage garnishment
Manitoba	70 per cent of your take-home pay is exempt from wage garnishment. A Manitoba wage earner is entitled to a minimum dollar amount of wages.
New Brunswick	Wage garnishments are not available in New Brunswick.
Newfoundland & Labrador	$649 in take-home pay is exempt from wage garnishment for a person with no dependants. A person who is supporting (1) a spouse or cohabiting partner and/or (2) one or more dependants will be entitled to significantly larger exemption.
Nova Scotia	85 per cent of your gross wages is exempt from wage garnishment. A Nova Scotia wage earner is entitled to a minimum dollar amount of wages.

Ontario	80 per cent of your take-home pay is exempt from wage garnishment
Prince Edward Island	The exemption amount is determined after a court official interviews the judgment debtor.
Quebec	70 per cent of your gross wages are exempt from wage garnishment. A Quebec wage earner is entitled to a minimum dollar amount of wages.
Saskatchewan	The exemption is $500 a month, plus $100 a month per dependent.

If you are self-employed and living in a Canadian province other than New Brunswick, you might find that you are not entitled to an exemption from a wage garnishment because the exemption is available only to salaried employees. If you are a real estate agent, for example, you might not be entitled to an exemption because your income comes from commissions and not wages. It is possible that a judgment creditor who serves a garnishment order on a real estate agent's broker might be entitled to 100 per cent of the commission a real estate agent would otherwise earn on a house deal.

PRACTICAL TIP

If you are self-employed and you live in a province other than New Brunswick, you might want to speak to a lawyer about your potential liability in the event that your creditor attempts to serve a garnishment order on someone who owes you money.

It might be possible in your province to seek an order from a judge (1) to grant you some kind of relief with respect to a garnishment order, for example, if you are a real estate agent or commission salesperson, or (2) to increase the wage exemption you are entitled to.

Garnishment of your bank account

Unless you live in New Brunswick, it is possible for a creditor who has successfully sued you to serve a garnishment order on the financial institution where you have a chequing or savings account and seize all the money in your account (but not more than what you owe under the judgment), assuming the account is solely in your name. Provincial law dealing with garnishment orders on joint bank accounts varies across Canada.

PRACTICAL TIP

If a creditor has obtained a judgment against you it might be prudent for you to avoid having money in your bank account, or for you to deposit just the minimum amount of money absolutely necessary at any particular time. Depending on which province you live in, you might want to consider opening a new joint account with your spouse, significant other, or close family member, where you can deposit *your* money, in order to limit your potential exposure to garnishment. Furthermore, your creditor can obtain a garnishment order on your savings or chequing account only if it knows the location of the specific branch where you have your account – another reason to keep your personal information secret.

If the money in your bank account is from social assistance payments, it might be illegal under provincial law for a creditor to obtain a garnishment order on your bank account. If this has happened to you, your creditor's actions may be illegal and you should contact a lawyer. Many provincial law societies have a lawyer referral service that enables you to speak to a lawyer for free for 20 to 30 minutes. You might also find it helpful to call the constituency office for your local member of the provincial legislature and make an appointment to explain your situation and seek assistance.

Placement of a lien on your real property

In some cases where a creditor has successfully sued you, it might place a lien on your real property. This is known as a *writ of execution*. Your creditor's goal is to obtain some or all of the money owing to it when you sell your home or you refinance it. No one will refinance your mortgage or purchase your property unless money owing under this writ of execution is paid out first.

THE RISK THAT YOUR PROPERTY MAY BE SEIZED AND SOLD

You may be concerned that your property could be seized in connection with an outstanding account. There are four scenarios in which this can happen:

1. If your creditor is a *secured* creditor and you default on your payment obligations, your creditor might seize its collateral (e.g., the lender from which you borrowed money to lease or purchase your car may repossess your car if you fail to make your payments).
2. If you have money in your account at a particular financial institution to which you owe money, your creditor can seize your money under the right of set-off without suing you first.
3. If you owe money to the Government of Canada, the federal government may "claw back" any money it owes to you such as income tax refunds or GST rebates.
4. If you owe money to an *unsecured* creditor who successfully sues you, your unsecured creditor might attempt to have some of your non-exempt property seized and sold.

It is very common for bill collectors to *threaten* consumers with unsecured debts that they will seize their property and sell it. But it is not very common for them to actually *do* it.

First of all, as you've learned by now, collection agencies do not sue people very often. Second, creditors typically prefer to use other enforcement remedies to recover money owing to them. It is expensive and time consuming for a creditor to seize personal property or real property using a *writ of seizure and sale of personal property* or a *writ of seizure and sale with respect to lands.* In Ontario, for example, it may be necessary to provide the Sheriff with a $5,000 deposit before the Sheriff will attend at a judgment debtor's residence to seize personal property.

Finally, a judgment creditor may not be able to satisfy a judgment by attempting to seize a judgment debtor's property because it may be exempt from seizure. In addition, the Sheriff may refuse to seize personal property unless he is satisfied no other creditors have a security interest in the personal property. This means that the Sheriff will be reluctant to seize your car because the company that lent you money when you leased or purchased it will almost always have a lien on it.

REASONS A JUDGMENT CREDITOR MIGHT ENCOUNTER PROBLEMS ENFORCING A JUDGMENT

There are nine reasons a judgment creditor might have trouble enforcing a judgment against you.

1. Your creditor cannot identify any assets or sources of income worth going after to satisfy a judgment

You may be working at a salaried job or be self-employed. Your name may be on title on your home or some other real property. You may have a chequing account or a savings account. Even still, if your creditor cannot locate these assets or income sources, it will not be able to use any of the enforcement remedies to recover money you owe it under a judgment.

2. You are judgment proof

You are considered *judgment proof* if your judgment creditor cannot recover any money from you even if you disclosed your assets and your sources of income. That could be the case if you fit into any of the following categories:

1. You support yourself on social assistance or a pension, and you do not own any significant assets, including any real property in which you have some equity.
2. You live in New Brunswick and you do not own any significant assets, including any real property in which you have some equity.
3. You have a job that you are prepared to quit if you are subject to a wage garnishment, and you do not own any significant assets, including any real property in which you have some equity.
4. You are working, 50 per cent of your wages are currently subject to a wage garnishment under court-ordered spousal support and/or child support payments, and you do not own any significant assets, including any real property in which you have some equity.
5. You are working, but in your province 100 per cent of your wages are exempt from garnishment because of an exemption protecting low-income wage earners from wage garnishment, and you do not own any significant assets, including any real property in which you have some equity.
6. Your personal property and real property are exempt from seizure, in whole or in part, under provincial law, which provides residents with certain protections from seizure of their property.

Each province in Canada has a law that exempts certain personal property and real property from seizure. These exemptions are not the same in each province. However, the law in each province typically contains a basic exemption of a few thousand dollars for household items such as clothing, furniture, and appliances. Most provinces have an exemption for an automobile up to a maximum of $3,000 to $5,000. Some provinces have an exemption for farmland, farm equipment, fishing equipment, and tools used by self-employed individuals to earn a living. In addition, some provinces, but not all, may have an exemption for land and/or a person's principal residence. For example, under provincial law Alberta residents are entitled to a $40,000 exemption from seizure with respect to their principal residence, but Ontario residents are not entitled to any. A detailed summary of these exemptions can be found on my website, www.helpwithcollectioncalls.ca.

3. You live in a province where low-income earners are effectively exempt from wage garnishments

In most, but not all, provinces low-income wage earners may be able to avoid wage garnishments, in whole or in part, because exemptions from wage garnishments provide for a minimum exemption, plus an additional exemption for their dependants. In Alberta, for example, if you are paid once a month, you are entitled to an $800 monthly exemption from a wage garnishment, plus a $200 exemption, per month, for each of your dependants. So if you earn $1,200 a month and have two dependent children, a creditor would not be able to recover any money from you under a wage garnishment. In contrast, in Ontario 20 per cent of an individual's take-home pay may be subject to wage garnishment regardless of how low that individual's wages are.

4. You quit your job if your wages become subject to a wage garnishment

One way to defeat a wage garnishment is to quit working for an employer who has been served with a wage garnishment order. This happens routinely. Unfortunately, some employees may also be fired, because their employer does not want the time, trouble, and grief associated with making payments into court. If you work for a large employer, the odds of your being fired because you are subject to a wage garnishment are extremely low. However, if you work for a small business there is a real possibility that you would be fired because your employer does not want to deal with the aggravation of the added paperwork necessary to honour a wage garnishment.

IMPORTANT FACT

It is illegal for your employer to fire you because it receives a wage garnishment notice.

5. Your wages are currently subject to a wage garnishment by other creditors or will be in the near future

Each province limits the size of the pot of money available to your creditors under one or more wage garnishments. From the perspective of your creditors, this pot will be even smaller if your wages are already subject to a wage garnishment, there are other outstanding judgments against you, or if you owe money to other creditors. In these cases it might take a long time for each creditor to satisfy its judgment, so they might be reluctant to sue you in an effort to obtain a wage garnishment. Furthermore, the fact that another creditor has already obtained a wage garnishment order against you means that any other creditor obtaining a wage garnishment order is going to have to share with other creditors from the dwindling pool of non-exempt money available to satisfy judgments.

PRACTICAL TIP

If you think your wages are going to become subject to a wage garnishment, and there is nothing you can do to prevent it, you may want to go out of your way to be nice to the person at your workplace who is responsible for preparing payroll. Maybe buy them a coffee or some doughnuts. This is particularly good advice if you work in the private sector and your employer has fewer than 50 employees.

6. You file for personal bankruptcy or make a successful consumer proposal

A wage garnishment against you will stop as soon as (1) you file for personal bankruptcy or (2) your creditors accept a consumer proposal. (A consumer proposal is a formal proposal to all of your unsecured creditors under which you propose to repay 25 to 50 per cent of all the money owing to them over three to five years.) Last year an Alberta resident arranged to become a debt settlement client with my law firm. I was unaware that five months earlier my new client had been served with a claim and a financial institution subsequently obtained a $19,000 default judgment against him. After my client's employer was served with a wage garnishment order, they suggested that he file for personal bankruptcy to stop the wage garnishment. The employer was correct: filing for bankruptcy would have stopped the garnishment.

Filing for personal bankruptcy can also defeat a creditor's writ of execution. Let's assume you own some real property. Your creditor has sued you and is in the process of filing a writ of execution against you in the jurisdiction where you own real estate in your name. If you file a successful consumer proposal or file for personal bankruptcy *before* your creditor files a writ of execution in the jurisdiction where your real property is located, your creditor's judgment is worthless. However, if your creditor files a writ of execution in the jurisdiction where your real property is located *before* you file for personal bankruptcy, your creditor's judgment will not be affected by your bankruptcy. This fact might be important to you if you own real property and your creditors have sued you.

PRACTICAL TIP

If you own real property and one or more of your creditors is in the process of obtaining judgments against you, it would be prudent for you to consider making a consumer proposal or filing for personal bankruptcy before your creditors have the opportunity to file a writ of execution in the jurisdiction where your real property is located.

7. You move to New Brunswick

If you were to move to New Brunswick, your creditor would not be able to take advantage of a garnishment order to do a wage garnishment, seize money in your bank account, or use any other type of garnishment.

8. You move to another country

This might be an extreme solution, but if you were to relocate outside of Canada you would make it that much more difficult and expensive for a creditor to recover money from you under a garnishment.

9. You seek judicial relief based on financial hardship

Depending on which province you live in, it may be possible for you to effectively defeat your judgment creditor if you can satisfy a judge that you would face financial hardship if a court failed to provide you with some measure of relief from an enforcement. You would need to show that a wage garnishment would have a serious negative effect on your finances. Most provinces permit a consumer whose wages are subject to a garnishment order to bring a motion before a judge and seek to have the exemption amount increased. Judgment debtors in Ontario have enjoyed the most success in doing so.

CHAPTER 10

REDUCING THE ODDS THAT YOU WILL BE SUCCESSFULLY SUED – AND WHAT TO DO IF YOU ARE

As noted earlier, if your outstanding account is sent to a collection agency it is unlikely that you are going to be sued. If you are going to be sued, it will mostly likely be by your creditor. The main focus of this chapter is to review those things you can do to reduce the odds you will be successfully sued, and at the end of this chapter we will also review the options available to you if you *have* been sued.

HOW TO REDUCE THE ODDS OF BEING SUED
There are a number of practical ways to do this.

Avoid speaking to a bill collector
If your goal is to avoid being sued, you should not speak to a bill collector. Period. They are trained to obtain all kinds of information from consumers that would be very helpful if the creditor decides to sue. Besides, nothing you can say to a bill collector will discourage a creditor from suing you except for the following:

1. You are not the debtor.
2. You dispute owing the debt.

3. You support yourself on social assistance.
4. You will be going for credit counselling or meeting with a bankruptcy trustee in the next three or four days.
5. You want your creditor to sue you because you have a counterclaim based on the creditor's conduct or the misconduct of a bill collector.

If you want to negotiate a settlement, you or your agent will want to speak to the creditor or its representative. When you do discuss a settlement with a bill collector, it is important that you not disclose any information about yourself.

Guard your personal information
Your creditor will be reluctant to sue you if it cannot identify a current home address or get your contact information. Your creditor will also be reluctant to sue you if it cannot identify any assets, employment income, or sources of income it could go after in order to satisfy a judgment against you.

Avoid acknowledging that you owe a debt
You should avoid doing anything to acknowledge owing a debt. Your creditor and its collection agent may be more interested in suing you if they know that you do not dispute owing an account, because the odds are higher that you won't defend a lawsuit. And if you do not defend the lawsuit, your creditor can obtain a default judgment against you in a relatively short period of time, and inexpensively. In contrast, if your creditor were to sue you and you were to file a defence, obtaining a judgment against you would involve more time, expense, and aggravation.

Avoid having money in your bank accounts
Your creditors may be encouraged to sue you if they can identify your bank accounts, because they may believe they will be able to seize money from these accounts.

PRACTICAL TIP

If your goal is not to be sued you should make all reasonable efforts to avoid having bank accounts solely in your own name.

In order to minimize the risk of having money in your bank account seized, you could do one of the following:

1. Have one or more bank accounts but keep as little money as possible in them.
2. Open a joint bank account with another person *whom you trust.*
3. Avoid maintaining any bank accounts at all.

If you have a joint bank account with another person, you run the risk that the other person will withdraw money from it. The law with regard to judgment creditors seizing money in joint bank accounts under a garnishment order varies across Canada. In some provinces a judgment creditor may be able to seize 50 per cent of the money in a joint bank account. Hundreds of thousands of Canadians do not have a bank account today. They typically cash any cheques they receive at a cheque cashing outlet, where they will be charged a significant fee for this service.

Incorporate your small business

If you are self-employed or you operate a small business, you might want to consider incorporating. This might provide you with some protection from creditors. An individual who owns a company is not personally responsible for the debts of the company. However, if your business is incorporated, your creditors may ask you to provide them with personal guarantees on credit they extend to your business. If you do this, you are agreeing to be personally liable for your company's debt, thereby forfeiting the advantage of incorporating a company. Wherever possible, you should avoid providing a personal guarantee.

I remember meeting with a couple who both owed a significant amount of money on their credit cards. The husband owned a trucking company, and he had provided personal guarantees in the tens of thousands of dollars to private individuals who had lent money to his business. His wife operated a successful hair salon that was a sole proprietorship. I suggested that she consider incorporating her salon so her creditors could not go after the income from it to pay for her personal debts.

Borrow money and use some of your existing assets as collateral
One of your judgment creditors' options is to seize some of your personal property or real property under a writ of seizure. This option may not be available to your creditors if the asset in question is already subject to a security interest by an existing secured creditor. So you can discourage an unsecured creditor from suing you by having some type of security interest placed on some or all of your property.

For example, if you own outright a car worth $15,000, you might want to borrow $10,000 from a lender, using the automobile as collateral. Your lender would place a lien on the car in the amount of $10,000. The fact that there is now a lien on the car would discourage an unsecured creditor from suing you. In most provinces approximately $5,000 in equity on an automobile is exempt from seizure. The bottom line is that your automobile cannot be seized as long as you repay the $10,000 loan. By making this loan, you have effectively removed this asset as a target for your unsecured creditors who have or who might obtain a judgment against you in the future.

Borrow as much money as you can using your real property as collateral
If you own real property and you have significant equity in your property, creditors might be motivated to sue you. One way to discourage them is to reduce the amount of equity that you have

in a particular property by borrowing money using your real property as collateral.

Avoid acting as a guarantor

A lot of people in this world get themselves into financial trouble by agreeing to act as a guarantor for the indebtedness of a friend or a family member. One of my own relatives, whom I will refer to as Martha, co-signed several loans for her daughter. The daughter was living in a large house that she and her husband could not afford. The daughter was self-employed and she was not making a go of it. Martha's daughter informed her that she could not handle the collection calls any more and was seriously considering bankruptcy. I explained to Martha that if her daughter defaulted on her debts, her daughter's creditors might sue her. Martha had lived a very frugal life, saved her money, and at age 68 owned her own home without a mortgage. Now she faced the prospect of losing her home because she had signed documents acting as a guarantor on her daughter's loans.

A WORD OF CAUTION ABOUT REVIEWABLE TRANSACTIONS

Sometimes individuals who are experiencing financial difficulties and are worried about being sued will do things that benefit certain individuals or creditors at the expense of others. Here are some examples:

- Giving away assets at a time when a person is insolvent
- Selling assets for less than the asset's market value
- Transferring assets into the name of another person such as a spouse or family member to protect them from creditors
- Paying off debts to some creditors but not to others

Certain transactions may be attacked as fraudulent (1) if they are made within a certain period prior to bankruptcy, (2) if they are made when you are insolvent, or (3) if you have organized your financial affairs for the express purpose of defeating your creditors. Any payments or transfers made within three months prior to filing for bankruptcy are reviewable. This three-month period is extended to 12 months in the case of transactions involving family members. Finally, this period may be extended to five years if at the time of the payment or transaction the debtor was insolvent or was unable to pay all of his creditors.

If you have made a fraudulent transfer the transaction may be attacked by a bankruptcy trustee or one of your creditors and the transaction may be reversed.

YOUR OPTIONS AFTER YOU HAVE BEEN SUED

Despite your best efforts to avoid being sued, it's possible that one or more of your creditors nevertheless will take this action. If they do, it would be prudent for you to speak to a lawyer at your earliest opportunity. It may be in your best interests to file a Defence or to take some other action in the next few days. A number of options are available to you *after* you have been sued:

1. Defend the lawsuit.
2. Negotiate a settlement with your creditor.
3. Seek judicial relief based upon financial hardship.
4. Make a consumer proposal or file for personal bankruptcy.
5. Do absolutely nothing.

If you have been sued it will usually, but not always, be necessary to file a defence so that you are not negotiating from a position of weakness. Once you are sued, the clock is ticking and you will be under time pressure to negotiate a settlement (covered in Part Four), unless you file a defence because at some point enough time will have elapsed, enabling your creditor to obtain a default judgment against you.

IMPORTANT FACT

If you are sued and your financial situation is dire, you may want to consider the merits of making a consumer proposal or filing for personal bankruptcy.

There are situations where it might make sense not to defend a lawsuit. This might arise where you support yourself on social assistance and you are judgment proof, and you have no legitimate defence. Your creditor will likely obtain a judgment against you but will be unable to enforce a judgment against you.

CHAPTER 11

THE CONSEQUENCES OF FAILING TO PAY YOUR ACCOUNT

In this section I've explained the many reasons that you might be able to avoid paying your outstanding accounts. Although you might be able to avoid paying your debt, doing so will have consequences, so it isn't a matter to take lightly.

YOUR ACCOUNT MAY BE IN COLLECTIONS FOR MANY YEARS

If you do not resolve your outstanding account, you should anticipate that it will be in collections for many years. When I was doing collection work we would attempt to collect outstanding accounts that were as old as 13 years.

YOU MIGHT BE SUED

If you do not pay your unsecured consumer debt, there is a chance you will be sued and your creditor will seek court costs, pre- and post-judgment interest, and legal fees in addition to the balance owing.

BORROWING MONEY MIGHT BE MORE DIFFICULT FOR YOU IN THE FUTURE

Large creditors almost always report your failure to pay a debt to one or both of Canada's two major credit reporting agencies, Equifax and TransUnion. This will have a negative impact on your credit score for the next six years. When you apply for credit, now or in the future, prospective lenders will look at your credit score from either Equifax or TransUnion. They will make the decision whether to lend you money, as well as at what interest rate, based on your credit score. The higher your credit score, the better, because this will make it less expensive for you to borrow money.

OTHER NEGATIVE CONSEQUENCES OF HAVING A POOR CREDIT RATING

There are a number of negative consequences to having a poor credit rating that are unrelated to borrowing money. These are set out in Mike Morley's book *The Complete Guide to Credit & Credit Repair for Canadians.* Employers may sometimes obtain a copy of your credit report as part of their hiring process, and if you have a bad credit report it may harm your chances of being hired. A poor credit report might make it harder for you to get security clearance for certain types of jobs, including those at senior levels in the government. Some utilities may require people with poor credit ratings to provide security deposits. In some cases insurance companies may refuse to insure people with a poor credit rating.

POTENTIAL INCARCERATION FOR BEING IN CONTEMPT OF COURT

In Canada people do not go to jail for failure to pay their debts. But it is possible for a judgment debtor to go to jail if she is served with a notice to attend at a judgment debtor examination and then she fails to attend. At a *judgment debtor examination* a representative from the judgment creditor asks a judgment debtor a series of questions regarding her financial situation, including income, expenses, and assets.

HOW TO RESOLVE YOUR OUTSTANDING DEBTS AND PROTECT YOUR CREDIT RATING

It is impossible to write a comprehensive guide for dealing with bill collectors without a review of the options available for handling your unsecured debt. Part Four will review these options in detail. Luckily, we don't have debtor's prisons in Canada, but you can still experience a tremendous amount of grief if you do not deal effectively with your debt situation. Depending on your financial position, you may be able to resolve your debts using one or more of the following:

1. Pay the entire balance owing in a single payment or in instalment payments (Chapter 12)
2. Settle a debt for less than the full amount owing by negotiating a lump sum payment (Chapters 13, 14, and 15)
3. Settle multiple debts using the Silverthorn Lite debt settlement strategy, in which you do not pay certain debts over a period of time, and then approach your creditors and negotiate favourable settlements, one after another (Chapter 16)
4. Employ the Silverthorn Max debt settlement strategy, in which you do not make any payments to certain unsecured

creditors before the expiry of a limitation period; after the limitation period has expired you decide whether you wish to settle any of your debts (Chapter 17)

5. Pay the entire balance owing using a debt management plan arranged through a credit counselling agency (Chapter 18)

6. Arrange for a consumer proposal or personal bankruptcy with a bankruptcy trustee (Chapter 19)

IMPORTANT FACT

If your debt is a government debt, as opposed to a consumer debt, your options for dealing with it will be more limited. It is difficult to negotiate a settlement with the government, and it will not agree to having the debt included in a repayment plan arranged through a credit counselling agency.

This section will cover each of your options for dealing with your debts. In Chapter 20, "Choosing the Appropriate Option for Resolving Your Debts," we will discuss those factors you should consider when charting your way forward, such as the precariousness of your financial situation, your credit score, and the cost of eliminating a debt.

PRACTICAL TIP

You should read Chapter 6 of this book before reading about your eight options for *eliminating* your outstanding debts. Depending on your particular financial situation, taking advantage of the expiry of a limitation period as a strategy for *avoiding* payment of a debt might be your best option.

CHAPTER 12

PAYMENT IN FULL AND INSTALMENT PAYMENTS

If you are receiving collection calls about an outstanding account, you might decide to resolve your debt by paying the entire amount owing. You have three options when it comes to paying a debt in full:

1. Payment in full: You pay the full amount owing with a single payment.
2. Instalment payments: You pay the entire amount owing with several payments over a period of time, typically providing a collection agency with a series of postdated cheques.
3. Repaying your unsecured consumer creditors through a repayment plan arranged by a credit counselling agency (see Chapter 18, "Debt Management Plan with a Credit Counselling Agency").

PAYMENT IN FULL

Collectors are trained to demand payment in full in the next few days when making their initial collection call. This deadline is just a date they pull out of thin air and is meaningless, because it is very unlikely you will be sued for not paying a debt within their time-frame. The same can be said for deadlines given in written notices from collection agencies.

Having said that, it might be in your best interest to pay in full, because it will protect your credit score better than any of the other options for dealing with your unsecured debts. After you make your payment, your credit report should be updated to show a balance of zero.

PRACTICAL TIP

If you legitimately owe a debt that has been in default for less than five months and you can afford to pay it, it is likely in your best interests to do so, especially if you will soon need to borrow large amounts of money at reasonable interest rates.

There are a number of situations in which you might not want to deal with an outstanding debt by paying it in full: if you have to borrow money at high interest rates to pay it, if the limitation period on your outstanding account is likely to expire in the next few months, or if you are in serious financial straits.

A collector may suggest that you make a payment in full by obtaining money from three potential sources: using your savings, borrowing money, or selling some of your assets to obtain the funds. Using your savings is straightforward, but before you borrow money or sell your assets, there are some things you should consider.

Borrowing money to pay a debt

Once you get that initial collection call, it is seldom in your best interests to borrow money in the next few days to pay your out-standing account. The collector is not motivated to do what is in your best interests. In fact, the collector is under tremendous pres-sure to encourage you to make payment in full in the next few days regardless of how this harms your financial situation. A collector who does not make her monthly quota may be fired.

PRACTICAL TIP
Do not let a collector pressure you into borrowing money to pay a debt in the next few days.

The most common explanation collectors hear for why a consumer cannot pay a debt is "I don't have the money." This is their cue for recommending a variety of ways you can borrow money, many of them at high interest rates. The collector may suggest you contact your credit card issuer and get your credit limit increased so you can obtain a cash advance, and then use the cash advance to pay the debt. A collector may also suggest you apply for a personal loan at a bank or finance company or borrow money using the equity in your home as collateral. Collectors routinely recommend that debtors borrow the money from family members or friends.

There are three important reasons you should avoid borrowing money to pay an outstanding account. First, the sky is not going to fall in if you do not pay the account this week, next week, or even six months from now. The odds that you are going to be sued for non-payment of your debt in the near future are relatively low. Even if you *are* sued, it is not the end of the world. Furthermore, some, but not all, chartered Canadian banks freeze the interest on a delinquent account when it is placed with a collection agency, whereas you might have to pay interest on any money you borrow. Finally, you may be in such a poor financial position that borrowing money to pay a debt could be the straw that breaks the camel's back.

If you are considering borrowing money to pay a debt, you should ask yourself what interest rate you will be paying on the borrowed money. Furthermore, you will want to know the total cost of borrowing the money to pay a debt. In the event you take out a personal loan, the total cost of borrowing money will include not only interest but also any life insurance premiums you have to pay. If you take out a mortgage on your residence, the total cost of borrowing will also include any legal fees you incur to arrange your loan.

You should avoid paying off a debt by obtaining a high-interest loan. This includes borrowing from a finance company, making a credit card payment, or taking out a cash advance on your credit card. You may actually put yourself in a worse financial position than before, because you are simply trading your current debt for another, which likely will have a much higher interest rate.

When you pay a debt in full, you pay 100 per cent of the amount owing and, in many cases, significantly more. If it is necessary for you to borrow money to pay your debt in full, you will incur added expense, not the least of which is interest costs. If you borrow money using a cash advance on your credit card or obtain a loan from a finance company, the real cost of eliminating a debt may be closer to 115 per cent or 130 per cent of the original debt. Because of the associated cost, paying a debt in full often does not compare very well with other debt elimination options.

If you owe thousands of dollars in credit card debt you may be paying a significant amount of interest on your outstanding balances. One option for those who wish to eliminate their credit card debt is to obtain a *consolidation loan*. Under a consolidation loan you borrow a sum of money, enabling you to pay off your existing high-interest-rate debt. A consolidation loan can be attractive if the interest rate on the consolidation loan is low. Unfortunately, not everyone is in a position to borrow enough money to pay off their high-interest-rate debt or to borrow the required money at a reasonable interest rate.

It may be in your best interest to obtain a consolidation loan if you can borrow money to eliminate an existing high-interest debt – provided the interest rate you are paying on the consolidation loan is significantly lower than the interest rate you are currently paying on your credit card debt. This is especially the case if your

continued ability to borrow large amounts of money is very important to you. For example, if you have no delinquent accounts,
except for a $2,000 credit card debt that is three months in default
and your mortgage is up for renewal in six months, you may save
thousands of dollars in future interest on your mortgage by paying
off your current credit card as soon as possible.

Selling some of your assets to pay a debt

A collector may suggest that you sell some of your assets, often
investments in an RRSP, to pay a debt. You should avoid taking
money out of your RRSP to pay a debt, because you will be
required to pay income tax on it. Even if you end up filing for personal bankruptcy, you will be able to keep your assets in your
RRSP, provided your contributions were made at least 12 months
beforehand.

INSTALMENT PAYMENTS

If you are receiving calls from a collection agency, you will usually
be able to pay the entire balance owing on your delinquent account
in instalment payments, that is, a series of payments over several
months or even years. Your goal in making instalment payments
is to pay your debt on *your* timetable instead of the collection
agency's. For many people, this is a much better option than
making a single lump sum payment because they can avoid borrowing money to pay the debt, thereby reducing the interest they
might have to pay.

There are two different scenarios for making instalment payments to a collection agency: you and the collector agree to a repayment schedule, the amounts to be paid, and the dates for each
payment (this is called *negotiated instalment payments*); or you
simply mail a series of postdated cheques to the collection agency
without the collector's knowledge or approval (*unilateral instalment payments*). You are less likely to receive future collection calls
in the former scenario.

PRACTICAL TIP
Making instalment payments may be an appropriate option for you to repay a debt owing to the government, because the government will rarely negotiate a settlement or agree to a repayment plan arranged through a credit counselling agency.

When you first inform a collector that you cannot afford to pay in full, you will typically be told to borrow money to pay your outstanding account. At this point, if you offer to make instalment payments, the collector will likely tell you that the collection agency will not accept instalment payments. This is not usually true. Trust me, if a collector is unable to persuade you to pay in full, at some future date the collection agency will be willing to discuss instalment payments.

When a collector is finally prepared to discuss instalment payments, her goal is to negotiate a repayment schedule that has the debt repaid as quickly as possible, preferably with a sizeable initial payment.

However, it is unnecessary for you to negotiate a repayment schedule. I don't care what a collector tells you. If you mail a series of postdated cheques to a collection agency, without the collector's knowledge or approval, the agency is going to cash your cheques – unless, of course, your cheques are for five cents each or they are being dishonoured. The collection agency might not like your timetable and you might continue to receive collection calls. However, there is little, if anything, it can do unless it wants to sue you in an effort to collect the debt more quickly.

The following example shows how a debt might be paid in instalments.

Bob owes $1,800 on his credit card with CountryBank. He is receiving collection calls from Acme Collection Agency. Bob offers to pay $1,800 over 18 months by providing 18 cheques for $100 each dated the first day of each month. The collector refuses to accept postdated *cheques and demands payment in full. Three months later this same collector agrees to accept instalment payments, provided the agency receives three postdated cheques for $600 each, dated 30 days, 60 days, and 90 days in the future. Bob declines this offer. Instead, he mails 18 postdated cheques worth $100 each to Acme Collection Agency, as he'd originally offered. Acme Collection Agency will cash these cheques. The agency may still make collection calls to Bob demanding repayment of the $1,800 over a period shorter than 18 months. However, it has no chance of getting its money more quickly unless it sues Bob.*

IMPORTANT FACT

It is unlikely you would be sued over your debt, but that is always a possibility. If you were, your instalment payments or postdated cheques could be used by your creditor as proof that you owe a debt. They could be seen as a written acknowledgement of the debt, restarting the clock on the limitation period.

If you choose to pay a debt using postdated cheques, you should make all reasonable efforts to ensure that you have sufficient funds to cover the cheques. One way to make a collector extremely angry is to send postdated cheques that bounce. You can reduce the chances of this happening by getting overdraft protection on your chequing account. If one of your cheques is returned NSF, you should try to provide the collection agency with a replacement cheque or money order as quickly as possible.

You should avoid sending postdated cheques to a collection agency for a period longer than 18 months because your situation may change during that time. You may move and change banks or bank branches and close your existing chequing account. Your financial situation may deteriorate, and you may no longer be able to make the payments. Alternatively, your financial situation may improve and you may want to pay the remaining balance off more quickly, with a new series of postdated cheques.

If you decide to pay your debt using instalments, you can use either a *conservative instalment payment strategy* or an *aggressive instalment payment strategy.*

Conservative instalment payment strategy

Under the *conservative instalment payment strategy* your goal is simply to pay one or more outstanding accounts using instalment payments, typically using a series of postdated cheques. One payment per month is the norm. The length of time you choose to make instalment payments will be determined by your cash flow situation. You can use this strategy to pay either your creditor or a collection agency.

Aggressive instalment payment strategy

The goal of an *aggressive instalment payment strategy* is to pay your debts in full as cheaply as possible using instalment payments, one creditor at a time, first paying those creditors who are continuing to charge you interest. Unlike the conservative instalment payment strategy, your accounts need to have been sent to a collection agency before you can begin making instalment payments under the aggressive instalment payment strategy.

This strategy has two important advantages. The first is the impact on your short-term cash flow situation. You are not going to be making instalment payments to a single creditor until some or all of your unsecured consumer debts have been forwarded to a collection agency, typically after six months. Second, it should be possible to reduce the total amount of your debt, provided at least one of your creditors freezes interest at the time your account is sent to a collection agency.

IMPORTANT FACT

If you use the aggressive instalment payment strategy, all of the accounts in question will attain an R9 rating and it will have a negative impact on your credit score.

The aggressive instalment payment strategy is a four-step process:

Step One: Default on certain unsecured consumer debts

The type of debts you would default on under an aggressive instalment payment strategy include credit cards, lines of credit, personal loans, and bank overdrafts. You have to exercise some common sense when choosing which debts to default on. If you do not pay rent on your apartment, you will be evicted. Similarly, if you do not pay the bill for your landline, cellphone, cable or Internet service, your service will be disconnected.

You also have to be careful defaulting on debts you owe to a financial institution that holds your chequing or savings account, because it might exercise the right of set-off and seize money from your bank account to pay off your debt. In some cases, it might be prudent for you to open a new bank account at a new financial institution and move all your personal banking there before you begin to default on your unsecured consumer debts.

PRACTICAL TIP

If you are unable to make the minimum monthly payments on *one* of your unsecured consumer debts, especially a credit card, you should probably default on *all* your unsecured consumer debts, so you can save the money to pay all your debts over time, using instalment payments. If you need the convenience of a credit card, you can always apply for a secured credit card.

Step Two: Determine if your creditor freezes interest on your delinquent account when it is sent to a collection agency

Think of your creditors as falling into one of two buckets. One bucket is for those creditors who continue to charge you interest on your outstanding account when it is sent to a collection agency. The second bucket is for your creditors, including some chartered banks, who freeze the interest on your outstanding balance when your account is forwarded to a collection agency.

If a creditor stops charging you interest, it will ultimately cost you less to repay the debt. So once your outstanding accounts are sent to a collection agency, you should determine which creditors are charging you interest on your outstanding balance and which are freezing the amount of interest owing.

PRACTICAL TIP
You can find out if interest is frozen on your account by calling a collector at the collection agency. Ask what your outstanding balance is today, how much of it is principal, and how much is interest. You can then ask how much will be owing at some future date, one, two, or four weeks in the future. If your balance owing four weeks from now is identical to your outstanding balance today, your creditor has frozen the interest on your outstanding account.

Step Three: Once your unsecured debts are six months in default, begin making instalment payments, one creditor at a time, to creditors who continue to charge interest
Once your debts are all six months in default, there is a good chance they have all been forwarded to a collection agency. Your first priority is to pay off debts that continue to accumulate interest. By doing this, you will reduce the total interest you end up paying. If more than one of your creditors continues to charge interest when it forwards accounts to a collection agency, you should prioritize your payments according to the interest rate: pay off the debt with the highest interest rate first.

Step Four: Pay those creditors who freeze interest
After you have paid in full those creditors who continue to charge interest on their outstanding balances, you can begin to make instalment payments to those creditors who freeze interest. The first creditor to be paid in full using instalment payments should be the one with the highest interest rate, and then the next highest, etc., until your debts are repaid.

Illustration of the aggressive instalment payment strategy
The following example will help illustrate the advantages of using
the aggressive instalment payment strategy to eliminate a debt.

*Let's say you have four credit cards, and your debts on them total
$18,000, as broken down in the following chart. In our example, you
are able to set aside $1,000 a month to make payments on your credit
card debt.*

Credit Card	Balance Owing	Interest Rate	Interest Accruing After Six Months In Default
A	$4,000	28%	Yes
B	5,000	9%	Yes
C	4,000	19%	No
D	5,000	9%	No
Total	$18,000		

*Under the aggressive instalment plan strategy you would not make
any payments on these four credit cards for the first six months.*

*By month seven all of your credit cards will have been in default for
six months and will have been placed with a collection agency. In
month seven you learn that of the four credit cards, interest is no longer
being charged on credit cards C and D. Therefore, your priority is to
pay off credit cards A and B, starting with credit card A, the card with
the highest interest rate, at 28 per cent a month. By now, you will have
saved $7,000 to pay off your credit cards, $1,000 in month seven and
$1,000 each in months one through six. Your balance on credit card
A is now $4,498, with interest, so you pay it off and reduce the balance
to $0. Of the $7,000 you have to repay your debts, you now have
$2,502 left, so you then make a $2,502 payment on credit card B, on
which interest is accruing at 9 per cent.*

*You would eliminate the remaining balance on credit card B by
paying $1,000 in month 8, $1,000 in month 9, and $766 in month
10. You now just have outstanding balances on credit cards C and D,*

and no interest is accruing on them, so there is less time pressure to pay them off. You reduce the balance on credit card C to zero in month 15 and on credit card D to $0 in month 20.

The total amount of interest you paid eliminating this $18,000 in credit card debt was $1,291 over an 20-month period.

Figure 4 summarizes the total amount of interest you would pay if you were to use $1,000 a month to pay off credit cards A, B, C, and D in our example under various instalment payment strategies, as well as debt consolidation loans.

Figure 4: Comparison of total interest paid on an $18,000 credit card debt

Repayment Method	Repayment Period	Total Interest
Instalments: Aggressive payment plan	20 months	$1,291.00
Debt consolidation loan at 14% interest	18 months	$2,323.67
Instalments: $250/month on all four cards	22 months	$2,646.00
Instalments: Pay high balance cards first	23 months	$3,215.00
Debt consolidation loan at 28% interest	18 months	$5,619.49

The least expensive method to repay this debt is the aggressive instalment payment plan strategy. The only way you can repay this $18,000 debt more cheaply is if you borrowed $18,000 at a very low interest rate, somewhere around 5 per cent.

Advantages and disadvantages of paying a debt in instalments
It may be to your advantage to pay a debt in instalments if you will not pay a significant amount of interest over the repayment period. Paying a debt by instalments can be very attractive to an individual who cannot borrow the money to pay off a debt or who can only borrow the money at a high rate of interest.

IMPORTANT FACT

You may find it cheaper to repay a debt using the aggressive instalment plan strategy than using a debt consolidation loan, unless you can obtain a debt consolidation loan at a very low interest rate.

Resolving your debts using instalment payments is not particularly attractive in circumstances where you are experiencing serious debt problems or if a significant percentage of your outstanding debt has a high rate of interest and interest will continue to accrue on your outstanding accounts after the debt has been delinquent for six months.

If you are in serious financial straits and your objective is to avoid insolvency, your objective should be either to avoid paying a significant percentage of your unsecured debts altogether or to eliminate your total debt as cheaply as possible, in which case some of your other options for resolving your debts will be superior to making instalment payments.

CHAPTER 13

SETTLING A DEBT

Wendy, a member of management at a university, owed $23,400 on her credit card. After she hired me in 2009, I contacted her credit card company and within nine months we settled this account for a payment of $3,300. Wendy saved more than $20,000 settling a single debt! Could Wendy have negotiated a settlement with this creditor on her own? Of course she could have, although she might not have been able to negotiate such a generous settlement, less than 15 cents on the dollar. Not every creditor is willing to settle its outstanding accounts for so little. However, if you take advantage of the advice in the next three chapters you will learn how to settle unsecured debts yourself, for anywhere between 20 cents and 35 cents on the dollar and some-times even less.

A collection agency's goal is to obtain payment in full from you. However, collection agencies routinely agree to settle debts for less than 100 cents on the dollar in a lump sum payment. As noted earlier, creditors typically send an overdue account to a collection agency when it is six months in default, or sometimes as early as three months. An overdue account has to be in default for several months before a creditor will be willing to settle a debt for less than the full amount owing.

There are two different scenarios for settling your debt, and the difference between the two arises because of the length of time you have to settle your debts. A settlement that you want to arrange in the next 90 days is one with a *short-term window of opportunity.* If you are willing to wait anywhere between 90 days and three years, and in some cases even longer, to settle your debt, you have a *long-term window of opportunity* in which to settle it.

There are a number of reasons you might want to settle your debt within the next 90 days. You might be trying to obtain a car lease or mortgage financing in the next 30 to 60 days and a potential lender has told you it will not lend you money unless you can prove that a particular debt appearing on your credit report is resolved. Or you might be receiving calls at your workplace from a collection agency, which is not only embarrassing but may also affect your job.

This chapter contains general information that is relevant whenever you are going to settle a debt for less than 100 cents on the dollar in a lump sum payment. Chapter 14 will be helpful if you are settling a purchased debt. Chapter 15 will help you settle a debt owned by your original creditor.

Chapters 16 and 17 will introduce you to a strategy for settling multiple debts, when you have a long-term window of opportunity. Using these *aggressive debt settlement strategies,* which I call Silverthorn Lite and Silverthorn Max, you might be able to eliminate one or more of your unsecured consumer debts for approximately 25 to 30 cents on the dollar, and sometimes even less. These strategies involve significant risks, and potential liability, and are definitely not for everyone.

WHICH TYPE OF DEBTS CAN YOU SETTLE?

You can usually negotiate lump sum settlements on unsecured consumer debt: credit cards, personal loans, lines of credit, and utilities (telephone bills, cable, Internet, and cellphone). You will find it difficult, if not impossible, to negotiate settlements with your secured creditors and with the government. However, you might be able to negotiate a settlement on a provincial student loan debt. In addition, you will likely be able to negotiate a settlement on a Canada Student Loan obtained between August 1, 1995, and July 31, 2000, in which case your creditor is a financial institution, and not the Government of Canada. Furthermore, you may be able to negotiate settlements with Canada Mortgage and Housing Corporation and 407 ETR, the private company that operates a major toll highway in southern Ontario.

You will find it difficult to negotiate a settlement on certain types of unsecured consumer debts. If you do not pay the rent on your apartment, your landlord can evict you. If you do not pay your landline, cellphone, cable, or Internet bills, these services will be terminated by your service provider.

SETTLEMENTS REQUIRE A LUMP SUM PAYMENT

IMPORTANT FACT

If you are going to settle an account for less than 100 cents on the dollar, you will need to make a lump sum payment.

Generally if you negotiate a settlement, you must make a lump sum payment, but sometimes you can make two or three payments over a 30-day period. You cannot negotiate a settlement for less than 100 cents on the dollar if you are making instalment payments to your creditor. If you can make only instalment payments on a debt, you will have to pay 100 per cent of the outstanding balance, and possibly interest. If your goal is to settle a debt for less than 100 cents on the dollar, the worst thing you can do is to make payments of any kind (unless you've received a written settlement offer and are making your lump sum payment).

A bill collector may try to get you to make a small payment as a token of your good faith in resolving your outstanding account. Don't fall for this ploy. If you make a small payment to your original creditor, this may result in a delay of several months in having your account sent to a collection agency, where a settlement for less than 100 cents on the dollar is available.

KEY FACTORS DETERMINING HOW MUCH YOUR CREDITOR WILL SETTLE A DEBT FOR

Your creditor will be more willing to negotiate a generous settlement with you

1. the longer your debt has been in default, or
2. if your creditor is satisfied that you are operating under a financial hardship and there is a good chance that you will never be able to repay a debt.

The length of time your account has been in default

You should not expect your creditor to be willing to settle your account for less than 100 cents on the dollar until your account has been overdue for a minimum of 6 to 12 months. Many large creditors will not consider settling an account for less than the total amount owing until it is at least 6 to 18 months in default.

You are experiencing financial hardship and will likely never be in a position to repay your debt

If your creditor is satisfied that you will likely never be able to repay 100 per cent of the money owing, it will be more willing to accept less than 100 cents on the dollar. The generosity of different creditors varies greatly. In fact, you might be able to obtain a generous settlement based, in whole or in part, on financial hardship when arguably the average person would not describe you as being a financial hardship case.

You should assume that when your creditor is deciding whether to make a generous settlement on the basis of financial hardship, it has a current copy of your credit report. The odds are low that your creditor will accept a settlement on the basis of financial hardship if your credit report discloses that you have sufficient credit available on your lines of credit or your credit cards to pay your outstanding debt in full. The following example will show you how to get around this.

A client of mine owed $12,000 on a student loan that he obtained from a major chartered Canadian bank. The bank was willing to settle for $10,000. When I was hired, my client had more than $15,000 available to him on his line of credit and two credit cards. My client actually worked for another major bank and his salary was more than $55,000 a year. There was no way we could successfully negotiate a settlement below $10,000 when my client's credit report showed he had $15,000 in credit available.

Our solution was to eliminate the $15,000 in available credit that appeared on my client's credit report. My client was able to do this by (1) making cash withdrawals on his line of credit, and (2) contacting his financial institutions and requesting a reduction in his available credit on both his line of credit and his credit cards. Three months later when I made a settlement offer to the collection agency representing the bank, my client had less than $2,000 in available credit appearing on his credit report.

I was able to settle this debt for a lump sum payment of $4,000 instead of the bank's original settlement offer of $10,000. I wrote a hardship letter for my client and provided the bank with a financial disclosure statement signed by my client, a copy of his recent pay stubs, and copies of his Notice of Assessment from Canada Revenue Agency for the two most recent taxation years. There were two key reasons the bank accepted my client's settlement offer of a $4,000 lump sum payment. First, his credit report showed that he had less than $2,000 *in available credit. Second, the hardship letter made a compelling case that if the bank were to decline this offer, it might never recover any money from my client.*

Your account is not owned by your original creditor
There is no guarantee that you can negotiate a generous settlement when your account has been sold to a debt buyer. I know of some cases where the owners of purchased debt refused to settle for less than 50 cents on the dollar. However, if they refuse to accept a generous settlement offer from you, they risk recovering nothing.

On the plus side, if a debt buyer does negotiate with you, you will be in a much stronger bargaining position than you would be in negotiations with your original creditor. Your original creditor usually has access to those documents that it would need to produce at trial to sue you successfully. In contrast, in most, but not all, situations, debt buyers will not be in a position to sue you, putting them in a poor bargaining position.

NEGOTIATING EFFECTIVELY
You can do a number of things to negotiate a debt settlement effectively:

1. Never forget about the big picture.
Last year an individual hired me to negotiate settlements for his unsecured debts. I felt pretty good after settling one of them for less than 15 cents on the dollar after my client's account had been in default for only six months. Two weeks later I got a frantic phone call from my client. He had received a letter from a lawyer representing the bank, informing him that they would be foreclosing on his home if he did not make a $4,000 payment within the next five business days. At no time before that had my client told me that he was in default on his mortgage payments.

IMPORTANT FACT
Your priority should be to put a roof over your head, put groceries on the table, and have funds available for any necessary transportation expenses, before you make payments on any outstanding debt. There is no point using your scarce dollars to eliminate your credit card debt for less than 20 cents on the dollar if you are going to be evicted from your apartment or lose your home.

2. Be clear about your objectives.

Establish some objectives. Is your goal to negotiate the best available settlement by a specific deadline? You might be under pressure to resolve one or more debts by a certain date because your mortgage is up for renewal or you want to obtain a car loan. Or is your goal to obtain the most generous settlement available? Maybe you are prepared to wait until your debt is 36 months in default, the date when the best settlements are usually available.

3. Find out if interest is continuing to accrue on your outstanding account.

For the first three to six months that your original creditor attempts to collect your account, it will be charging you interest on your outstanding balance. As noted earlier, some creditors will stop charging interest on your overdue account when they send it to a collection agency. Once your account has been forwarded to a collection agency, it is very helpful to determine if interest has been frozen or is continuing to accrue.

If interest is not accruing on your outstanding balance, you can afford to be patient while waiting to settle your outstanding account. However, if you owe money on a credit card with a very high interest rate and interest is not frozen, you might want to act sooner than later to try to resolve this outstanding account.

4. Obtain a current copy of your credit report.
You might find it helpful to have a current copy of your credit report in front of you when you are speaking with a bill collector, particularly if you're trying to settle an overdue account on the grounds that you are experiencing financial hardship. After all, the bill collector might very well be doing the same. To learn how to obtain a current copy of your credit report, see Chapter 2, "What You Should Know About Your Credit Score and Your Credit Report."

5. Determine when your account will be recalled by your creditor.
If you are receiving collection calls from a collection agency, it is likely collecting your account on a commission basis (unless it has purchased your account). If so, the agency might be more likely to make a generous settlement with you during the last 30 days before your account is recalled by your creditor. One of your objectives should be to try to determine when your account will be recalled. A collector might disclose this information to you.

6. Be patient.
When it comes to settling debts, patience is a very important virtue. A collection agency will typically have your account for anywhere between 6 and 12 months. Initially, it will attempt to obtain payment in full from you. As time goes by, it will likely be more interested in settling your account for less than 100 cents on the dollar.

PRACTICAL TIP
To obtain the most generous settlement available, avoid settling a debt during the first 90 days it has been placed with a collection agency.

OBTAINING A WRITTEN SETTLEMENT OFFER

IMPORTANT FACT

You should never settle an outstanding account before receiving a settlement letter that is acceptable to you. Do not make a payment until you have received this letter, and once you make a payment, keep a copy of this settlement letter in a safe place, along with your proof of payment.

It is very common in the collection industry for a creditor to send an account to a second collection agency after it was settled by the first collection agency. If you receive collection calls on an account after you've settled it, you can simply fax the new collection agency a copy of your settlement letter and your proof of payment and you should not hear from it again. If the collection agency continues to make payment demands after you provide proof of payment, it is violating provincial law regulating collection agencies for attempting to collect a debt from someone who does not owe a debt.

By making a payment to your creditor or its collection agent before you receive a satisfactory written settlement letter, you run the risk that your creditor will demand additional money from you at some future date. Unethical collectors may also generate a significant number of payments from consumers by making verbal settlement offers for ridiculously low amounts when the creditor has not authorized settlements at these amounts.

The following example illustrates the grief consumers can face when they do not obtain a settlement offer before making a payment to a collection agency.

Jim does not have any outstanding accounts other than $10,000 owing to Bank X. After this account has been in default for six months, Bank X places Jim's account for collection with ABC Collection Agency. A collector from ABC Collection Agency calls Jim and informs him that

Bank X will accept $3,000 as settlement in full provided the $3,000 payment is received by the collection agency within five business days. Jim cannot believe his good fortune, so he borrows the money from his brother and makes the $3,000 payment within the five days. Jim did not ask for nor did he receive a written settlement letter from ABC Collection Agency offering to settle this debt for a lump sum payment of $3,000.

Three months later Jim receives a collection letter from Acme Collections demanding a $7,000 payment on his outstanding account with Bank X. Jim is upset, so he phones Acme Collections and advises them that he settled this account three months ago for a lump sum payment of $3,000. Jim receives a call two months later from Acme Collections. Jim is advised that neither Bank X nor the previous collection agency, ABC Collection Agency, have any record of a settlement for $3,000. Furthermore, Jim is advised that any settlements below $10,000 would have had to be approved in writing by a Bank X employee. There is no record of ABC Collection Agency making a request to Bank X for a settlement offer of any kind on his account.

Jim has likely been the victim of an unethical collector. Jim could have avoided this entire fiasco by simply insisting on receiving a settlement letter from ABC Collection Agency before making his $3,000 payment. If ABC Collection Agency is a large collection agency, it is possible that the agency records its collection calls, in which case Jim can attempt to obtain a copy of the telephone conversation in which the settlement offer took place. If Jim cannot obtain a copy of the conversation, he faces the prospect of further collection activity and a potential lawsuit.

Regardless of whether you are settling an account with your original creditor, a debt buyer, a lawyer, or a collection agency, you should receive a satisfactory settlement letter before making your payment. It can be sent to you by fax, mail, Xpresspost, or courier. Due to privacy concerns, a collection agency will rarely e-mail you a settlement offer.

When you receive a settlement offer, read it carefully. The letter should be on the company's letterhead and contain your name, properly identify the account in question, and state that the payment of a specific dollar amount will be accepted as settlement in full. The letter should be signed by the company's representative and state the name and title of the person signing the letter. A settlement letter will usually state that the offer will expire if the payment is not received at the firm's office by a certain date.

AVOID MAKING A WRITTEN SETTLEMENT OFFER TO A COLLECTION AGENCY

IMPORTANT FACT
If you are having settlement discussions with a collection agency, request a settlement letter from it. You should avoid sending a collection agency a settlement letter yourself.

Collection agencies routinely send out settlement letters. They expect consumers to request them. If you do the reverse and send a collection agency a settlement letter, you run the risk of it being (1) used as a written admission that you owe the debt at trial, and (2) a written acknowledgement that you owe the debt, which would restart the clock on the statute of limitations. The fact that you verbally request a collection agency to send you a settlement letter is not going to prejudice you in any way.

Unless the debt is a large amount or the legal issues involved are complex, there are a number of reasons it is probably not a good idea to have your lawyer draft a settlement letter either. First of all, you will incur the cost of your lawyer drafting the release document. Second, there is a good chance that no one from the collection agency will be willing to sign it. Collection agencies have one or possibly two standard settlement letters that they use, perhaps hundreds of times each day. There is a good chance that no one at the collection agency, other than perhaps a senior collection manager, has authority to sign a release letter drafted by your lawyer. Collection agencies are bureaucracies that may refuse to deal with any forms other than their standard ones.

It might, however, be prudent for your lawyer to read the collection agency's settlement letter and to give you advice about whether it is acceptable for you to forward your payment to the agency in response to the settlement letter.

SETTLING A DEBT AT THE END OF THE MONTH

If you go to a car dealership on the last two days of the month, you might be able to get a better deal on a new car if your salesman has not met his sales quota for the month. Like car salesmen, collectors have a quota on commissions they are supposed to generate, and since collection agencies are constantly in competitive races with rival collection agencies, by the end of the month collectors are often under a lot of pressure to resolve outstanding accounts. Each day that month-end draws nearer, this pressure increases. Collectors will feel the most pressure to settle an account on the last day of a calendar month. In order for you to obtain the most generous settlement available, the collection agency must be in a position to receive your payment on or before the last business day of a calendar month.

PRACTICAL TIP

You will often be able to get a more generous settlement from a collector employed by a collection agency during the last five business days of a calendar month than you can earlier in the month.

In order to negotiate the best available settlement, you should not wait until the last day of the calendar month to speak to a collector at a collection agency. By then it is probably too late. You have to take into consideration two factors: (1) the length of time it will take the collection agency to send you a written settlement letter, and (2) whether you can get money to a collection agency by the end of the calendar month.

Most large collection agencies have a trust account at one or possibly two of the large chartered banks. You can usually get your payment to the collection agency by its month-end deadline by going to the financial institution in person and making a cash deposit or making a payment using a money order, bank draft, or certified cheque payable to the agency or the creditor.

SETTLING A DEBT IN THE LAST TWO WEEKS IN DECEMBER

The best time of year to negotiate a generous settlement is during the last two weeks in December. Historically, December is the month when collection agencies bring in the least revenue. In fact, it is very common for collection agencies to lay off significant numbers of support staff in December in an attempt to avoid operating at a loss for the month.

OBTAINING A SECURED CREDIT CARD

In some instances, negotiating settlements will involve your not paying one or more of your creditors for a significant period of time. If you stop making payments on all your credit cards, you will be left without the convenience of a credit card, which can be challenging in the modern world. Not having a credit card can make it very difficult to rent a car or a hotel room or order a book or concert tickets online.

If you are going to stop making payments on one or more of your credit cards, you should consider obtaining a secured card with a modest credit limit of $500 to $2,000. This is a credit card with a prepaid balance that offers all the convenience of an unsecured credit card. You can obtain an application for one of these cards at a Money Mart outlet or through the following companies:

Royal Bank
ATB Financial
Capital One
Home Trust
Peoples Trust
Vancity Credit Union

SETTLING A DEBT AND YOUR CREDIT REPORT

You will recall that you will not be able to settle a debt until it is at least six months in default, by which time it attains an R9 rating on your credit report, the worst there is. Your credit report lists the dollar amount owing on a specific item. When an account is resolved through a settlement, the dollar amount is updated to zero and noted as settled in full. When your account is resolved through a settlement, the impact on your credit rating is comparable to that of credit counselling or a consumer proposal.

CHAPTER 14

SETTLING A DEBT OWNED BY YOUR ORIGINAL CREDITOR

Nine out of ten accounts that collection agencies attempt to collect today are owned by the original creditor that provided you with goods, services, a loan, or some form of credit. Large creditors in Canada typically try to collect overdue accounts on their own for three to six months before forwarding them to a collection agency. During that period, your creditor will rarely be willing to settle your account for less than the full amount owing.

PRE-APPROVED SETTLEMENT INSTRUCTIONS
When a creditor first sends your overdue account to a collection agency, the creditor will provide instructions to the agency regarding your account. There are two different scenarios:

1. Your creditor could instruct the collection agency to collect 100 per cent of the outstanding balance and the agency will be given no authority whatsoever to settle it for less than 100 cents on the dollar.
2. Your creditor could provide the collection agency with authority to settle your account in accordance with

pre-approved settlement instructions. Your creditor might, for example, authorize the agency to settle your overdue account for 85 cents on the dollar.

If you owe $10,000 and your client's pre-approved settlement instructions are 85 per cent, the collection agency has the authority to settle your account for a lump sum payment of $8,500. But don't expect a collection agency to just phone you up and tell you exactly what is the most generous settlement available under the pre-approved settlement instructions provided by its client.

Individual creditors establish their pre-approved settlement instructions internally. One creditor's settlement instructions might be significantly different from another's. A major financial institution, for example, may have different pre-approved settlement instructions for different product lines: one for credit cards, one for personal loans, and one for lines of credit. A financial institution might even have several different pre-approved settlement instructions that apply to different classes of credit cards they offer to the public. The fact that the limitation period on your account will soon expire or has expired is not a significant factor in a creditor's determining your pre-approved settlement instructions.

A collection agency that initially gets your file will typically have your account for 6 to 12 months. During the initial half of this period, the collection agency will try to obtain payment in full from you. However, during the latter half, the collection agency may be happy to discuss a lump sum settlement with you. Remember, though, that a collection agency may exhaust its efforts to collect 100 per cent of the outstanding balance from you before it will be interested in settling your account for less than 100 cents on the dollar.

If you ask a collector during your first telephone conversation if you can negotiate a settlement for less than 100 cents on the dollar, the collector is highly unlikely to admit that it is possible. She might say something like "Some creditors might settle their accounts, but not this one. I only have your account till next Friday. If I don't have payment in full in my office by 4 p.m. next Friday you will be sued. Would you prefer to be served with a statement of claim at home or at work?"

As noted in Chapter 1, when a large creditor sends your account to a collection agency, it is referred to as a *first assign*. When your account is a first assign, the collection agency might have authority to settle your account for a lump sum of less than 100 cents on the dollar, typically around 85 cents on the dollar.

IMPORTANT FACT
The longer your outstanding account is overdue, the more generous the settlements are likely to be.

Your unpaid account will often remain as a first assign for about 12 months, at which time it will be recalled by the client and then sent to a new collection agency as a *second assign*. If your creditor's pre-approved settlement instructions on a first assign was 85 cents on the dollar, on a second assign it might be 65 cents on the dollar. After your account has been with a second collection agency for 9 to 12 months, it will typically be recalled by your creditor and sent to another collection agency as a *third assign*. Once your account is 24 months in default, the pre-approved settlement instructions on your account may be reduced to 50 cents on the dollar.

Your unpaid third assign will typically be recalled after six to nine months. At this point it will be referred to as another third assign, or in some cases a *fourth assign*. By the time your outstanding account is 36 months in default, your creditor might be willing to settle your outstanding account for an amount between 20 and 35 cents on the dollar, and sometimes even less. The pre-authorized settlement instructions will not typically be reduced any further after 36 months.

Figure 5 is designed to give you some sense of how major creditors in Canada today will negotiate lump sum settlements. These figures are not exact.

Figure 5: Estimates of settlements available from your creditor

Time That Your Account Has Been in Default	Amount Creditor Wants to Receive on Your Account
Less than 6 months	100 cents on the dollar
6–12 months	Between 85 cents and 100 cents on the dollar
12–18 months	85 cents on the collar
18 months	65 cents on the dollar
24 months	50 cents on the dollar
36 months	20–35 cents on the dollar

MORE GENEROUS SETTLEMENTS THAN THOSE PERMITTED UNDER PRE-APPROVED SETTLEMENT INSTRUCTIONS

In certain circumstances, it might be possible to obtain a lump sum settlement that is more generous than even the most generous settlement permitted under a creditor's pre-approved settlement instructions. These kinds of settlements are usually available only when the creditor is satisfied that the consumer will never be in a financial position to repay a debt in its entirety. People who might fall into this category include those who are supporting themselves on social assistance or those who have experienced health problems that are affecting their ability to work and earn a living.

A collection agency has no authority to settle your account for an amount less than the creditor's pre-approved settlement instructions. A collection agency needs to request permission from your creditor to settle your account for a specific amount that is more generous than the creditor's pre-approved settlement instructions. This is done on a case-by-case basis.

For a creditor to consider a settlement that is more generous than its pre-approved settlement instructions, it will usually require the consumer to disclose significant details about his financial situation. Your creditor will probably require the following information:

1. Completion of its financial disclosure form listing your assets, liabilities, income, and monthly living expenses
2. Two recent pay stubs
3. A copy of your Notice of Assessment from Canada Revenue Agency for the past two years
4. A signed hardship letter explaining why you will likely never be in a position to repay a debt in full

CHAPTER 15

SETTLING A PURCHASED DEBT

In 2009 one of my clients sent me a collection letter he'd received from a lawyer working on behalf of a debt purchaser. You can tell his debt has been purchased, because the first sentence read this way:

I have been retained to collect from you money owed to Resurgent Capital Services to whom you are indebted in the amount of $_____ for the debt formerly owing to Wells Fargo Canada.

My client may or may not have dealt with Wells Fargo Canada at some point in time. My client, however, certainly never obtained goods or services or borrowed money from a U.S.-based company named Resurgent Capital Services.

TWO CATEGORIES OF DEBT PURCHASERS IN CANADA

As noted earlier, your original creditor can sell your debt to another company called a debt purchaser, often for no more than a few pennies on the dollar. There are two different types of debt buyers: traditional collection agencies and *dedicated debt purchasers*. The latter are companies whose primary business involves buying thousands of unpaid accounts from large creditors and then sending these accounts to collection agencies for collection on a commission basis. Collection agencies buy a significant percentage of all the purchased debt collected in Canada.

The following chart shows the difference between a traditional collection agency and a dedicated debt purchaser, both of whom buy purchased debt.

Figure 6: Comparison of a traditional collection agency with a dedicated debt buyer

CHARACTERISTIC	TRADITIONAL COLLECTION AGENCY	DEDICATED DEBT BUYER
Purchases debt	Sometimes	Always
Collects money for others on commission	Always	Never
Employs collectors	Always	Seldom

IDENTIFYING WHEN YOUR ACCOUNT IS A PURCHASED DEBT

A number of red flags will help you to identify a purchased debt. First of all, you might never have heard of the creditor to which the bill collector claims you owe money. Second, the collector makes *reference to two creditors,* a company to which you would appear to currently owe money, plus your original creditor. Finally, you might not remember owing the debt described in a purchased account because they are often several years old, possibly five or ten, and sometimes older.

You should be able to determine if a debt has been purchased by looking at the collection letter. Figure 7 explains how to read between the lines to find out who owns your debt. If your original creditor has sold your debt, the purchaser is legally required to inform you that it is not your original creditor.

Figure 7: References to creditors in a bill collector's demand letter

DEBT OWNED BY	REFERENCES TO CREDITORS IN THE DEMAND LETTER
Original creditor	Money owing to original creditor
Collection agency	A debt owing to the collection agency, a former debt of the original creditor
Dedicated debt buyer	Money owing to dedicated debt buyer, a former debt of the original creditor

SETTLING A PURCHASED ACCOUNT

Let me walk you through the various steps of settling a purchased debt:

Step One: Look at your credit report and confirm that this account appears on it

As far as the world is concerned, a debt does not exist if it does not appear on your credit report. When you resolve an account that does not appear on your credit report, the action has zero impact on your credit score. Furthermore, credit reporting agencies normally remove items from your report when the date of last payment is more than six years ago.

PRACTICAL TIP

If a purchased debt does not appear on your credit report, I recommend that you *not* pay the account.

Step Two: Satisfy yourself that this is a legitimate debt that you really owe

If this account *does* appear on your credit report, you should satisfy yourself that it is a legitimate debt. When bill collectors are collecting purchased debt, there is always a possibility that they have the wrong person or, in some cases, the incorrect amount owing. And while it is illegal and almost unheard of for a creditor to falsely put a derogatory notation on a person's credit report, it is very common for creditors to put incorrect information on an individual's credit report in error.

If the bill collector cannot provide you with documentation proving that you owe the debt, it will probably never be able to successfully sue you.

I would not normally suggest that you attempt to settle a purchased debt that appears on your credit report if the debt buyer cannot prove you owe the debt. In this situation, you might want to consider having a lawyer write a letter threatening to sue the creditor for defamation as well as filing a complaint with regulators over your creditor making false reports on a credit report. There is a possibility that a debt buyer has listed a purchased debt on your credit report in a situation where it is illegal for it to do so.

Step Three: Negotiate a settlement
Now you're ready to negotiate your settlement, so let me walk you through the various steps.

1. Determine when you made your last payment on this account and when the statute of limitations will expire.
Ideally, you should figure out (1) the date of last payment on this account or (2) the date of any written document that you signed and gave to the original creditor, its agent, or the debt purchaser acknowledging your indebtedness for this account.

You should also ask yourself (1) whether the relevant limitation period on this debt has expired, and (2) if it has yet to expire, when it will expire. See Chapter 6 for more information on limitation periods.

2. Refuse to discuss a potential settlement with a bill collector until the collector makes you a settlement offer.
You should refuse to discuss a potential settlement with the collector until he first makes you a settlement offer. You will gain an advantage in the negotiations if you get the bill collector to make a settlement offer before you do.

3. Make a lowball settlement offer.
Your goal should always be to settle a purchased debt for as little as possible. You are, therefore, never going to pay 100 per cent of the amount the bill collector claims you owe on a purchased debt unless the debt purchaser successfully sues you. Make no mistake: the debt purchaser does not want to sue you. Therefore, it is important for you to be patient and wait for the collector to make you a settlement offer before you make your lowball settlement offer. Don't forget that the clock is ticking on the statute of limitations. The closer you are to the expiry of a limitation period, the stronger your bargaining position.

PRACTICAL TIP
After a bill collector has made you a settlement offer, I recommend that you verbally make a lowball offer and advise the collector that it expires within 20 business days.

A lowball settlement offer would be five or ten cents on the dollar, unless your account is only 6 to 18 months in default, in which case a lowball offer should be between 25 cents and 35 cents on the dollar. The bill collector will reject your offer, but it may encourage him to reduce his original offer.

The bill collector will either accept your offer, decline to accept your offer, or make a counteroffer. If your offer is not accepted, you might choose to take a *hardline position*. When you take a hardline position, you simply advise the bill collector to call you if he changes his mind about your offer.

If your offer is not accepted, you might choose to take a more flexible bargaining position. When you adopt a *flexible position,* your first offer is not your best offer. If your offer is not accepted, you can inform the collector you are willing to settle for an amount that is 5 per cent or 10 per cent higher than your original lowball offer. It is important when you adopt a flexible position during negotiations that you are not bargaining against yourself. You should not be indicating a desire to settle this purchased debt at a higher percentage if the other side is not also reducing the amount it is seeking.

CHAPTER 16

THE SILVERTHORN LITE DEBT SETTLEMENT STRATEGY

In Chapter 13 you learned some of the basics of debt settlement. In Chapter 14 we explored settling a debt owned by your original creditor, and in Chapter 15 we covered settling a debt when your original creditor has sold your account. In this chapter you are going to learn an aggressive strategy for settling one or more debts, which I refer to as the Silverthorn Lite debt settlement strategy.

The goal of the Silverthorn Lite debt settlement strategy is to enable you to eliminate one or more of your unsecured consumer debts for approximately 20 to 35 cents on the dollar, and sometimes less, using a single lump sum payment. In order to obtain the most generous settlements available, you will usually have to wait until your account has been in default for 24 to 36 months.

There is no guarantee that if you execute the Silverthorn Lite debt settlement strategy you will be able to obtain these results, particularly if you are sued. We will review some of the limitations of this strategy in more detail later in this chapter.

IMPORTANT FACT
You may want to consider using the Silverthorn Lite debt settlement strategy if (1) you are experiencing difficulties making the minimum payments on your credit cards, personal loans, or lines of credit or (2) you owe more than $10,000 in unsecured consumer debt.

If you are experiencing significant financial difficulties, the Silverthorn Lite debt settlement strategy can be superior to a debt consolidation loan, credit counselling, a consumer proposal, or personal bankruptcy. In particular, it should be particularly attractive to (1) residents of Ontario, Alberta, Saskatchewan, and Quebec, where limitation periods on consumer debt are only two or three years, and (2) people who do not owe significant amounts of money to the government.

The Silverthorn Lite debt settlement strategy is a three-stage process. Stage One consists of planning and preparation. In Stage Two you stop making payments to selected unsecured creditors and amass a *debt settlement war chest,* funds available for future lump sum settlements. This can take quite some time. In Stage Three, which may last several years, you settle one unsecured debt at a time, typically biding your time waiting for the best opportunity to make a generous settlement with a specific creditor.

STAGE ONE: PLANNING AND PREPARATION
In Stage One of the Silverthorn Lite debt settlement strategy, you will need to do the following:

1. Establish specific objectives.
2. Make any arrangements to secure access to credit.
3. Make any necessary banking arrangements.
4. Make arrangements to obtain money for your debt settlement war chest.
5. Develop a plan for dealing with collection calls.

1. Establish your objectives.

Before you use the Silverthorn Lite debt settlement strategy, you will need to establish some specific objectives. First, you should list your unsecured current debts, then identify the debts suitable for settlement, and determine how much money you have available for dealing with your current debt situation. Mike's situation below will help illustrate how this strategy works.

Step One: List all your unsecured debts.

List all of your unsecured debts.

Mike has the following debts.

Credit card A	*$10,000*
Credit card B	*$7,500*
Credit card C	*$2,500*
Line of credit A	*$7,500*
Line of credit B	*$2,500*
Personal Loan	*$5,000*
Outstanding income taxes with Canada Revenue Agency	*$5,000*
Total	*$40,000*

Step Two: Determine how much money you have available each month to deal with your unsecured debts.

When you are determining how much money you have available to deal with your unsecured debts, exclude money you currently devote to (1) monthly living expenses, such as shelter and food costs, and (2) financial obligations related to your secured debts, such as car payments and mortgage payments. Take into consideration the fact that you will no longer be able to use credit to maintain your current standard of living.

Mike is currently paying about $1,500 a month to service his unsecured debts. He does not anticipate his income changing in the future, and he *can't continue to use credit to maintain his standard of living. Under the circumstances, it will be prudent for Mike to set aside $1,000 a month to deal with his $40,000 in debts.*

Step Three: Identify those debts that you are not going to resolve using debt settlement.
There are some debts that you cannot resolve using debt settlement and some that you might prefer not to deal with using debt settlement. For instance, you cannot usually settle a debt owing to the federal government because it wants 100 per cent of the outstanding balance plus interest and penalties. You will likely not want to resolve a debt using debt settlement if

1. money is owing to your employer,
2. you owe money to a friend or family member, or
3. your friend or family member acted as a guarantor for your indebtedness.

Of Mike's $40,000 debt, the $5,000 in income tax owing to Canada Revenue Agency cannot be resolved through debt settlement. Therefore, Mike has $35,000 in unsecured consumer debt that he can resolve using the Silverthorn Lite debt settlement strategy.

Step Four: Develop a plan for dealing with debts you are going to resolve through debt settlement and debts for which you are not going to use debt settlement.
Before you determine how you are going to resolve debts through debt settlement, you should consider how to handle your other debts.

Mike will have $1,000 a month available to deal with his unsecured debts. Mike has $40,000 in debt, $5,000 of which he owes to the federal government in income taxes. Mike has a number of options for dealing with his income tax debt. He can make monthly payments or he can do nothing and hope that the federal government will claw back this *debt using any future income tax refunds or GST rebates he is entitled to.*

If Mike were to make 24 monthly instalments of $275, an amount totalling $6,600, this amount should be sufficient to eliminate his $5,000 debt to the federal government, a debt for which he will pay interest and penalties. If Mike has $1,000 available to deal with his debts and $275 a month will be used for his income tax debt, he is left with $725 that he can save in his debt settlement war chest to eliminate his $35,000 in consumer debt. If Mike has $35,000 in unsecured consumer debt that he is going to settle using the Silverthorn Lite debt settlement strategy, he should save an amount equal to 50 per cent of $35,000, or $17,500. If Mike contributes $725 a month into his debt settlement war chest, he will save more than $17,500 in 25 months.

Once you have decided the amount of debt you want to settle using the Silverthorn Lite debt settlement strategy, you should devise a plan for saving 50 per cent of this amount, taking into consideration (1) the total amount of money you have available to deal with your unsecured debts, and (2) the amount of money you will require each month to resolve debts by other means.

You might have noticed that I suggest you save 50 per cent of your unsecured debt when earlier I told you that you should be able to negotiate settlements for 20 to 35 cents on the dollar and sometimes less. There are several reasons that I suggest you save an amount equal to 50 per cent:

1. It is possible that you will skip a monthly payment from time to time due to unforeseen expenses.
2. You might be sued on one of your accounts and if you were to settle this account by paying it in full, you will need the additional money. If your creditor goes to the time, trouble, and expense of suing you, your creditor may not be interested in a settlement period or your creditor might be prepared to accept 80 or 90 cents on the dollar, payable within the next 30 days.

3. You may decide to hire someone to negotiate debt settlements on your behalf, in which case you will need to pay them some fees.

If you are able to set aside an amount equal to 55 per cent or 60 per cent of the total amount of debt, that would be even better.

2. Make any arrangements to secure access to credit.
You might need to use the Silverthorn Lite debt settlement strategy for several years. You may find it difficult to obtain credit during this period. This means that it would be prudent for you to have access to a line of credit, or possibly a credit card with a limit between $500 and $2,000, primarily for emergency purposes, or for those times of the year when you have a number of extraordinary expenses.

If you stop making payments on all your credit cards or lines of credit, you will lose those privileges. If you want to have access to credit during the period in which you are taking advantage of the Silverthorn Lite debt settlement plan, you have a couple of options:

1. Do not default on one of your existing credit cards or lines of credit.
2. Before you start defaulting on your unsecured debts, apply for a new credit card or line of credit at a financial institution where you do not currently bank.

If you do decide not to deal with an existing credit card or line of credit in order to have access to credit during the period you employ this strategy, you will likely need to revise the amount of money you will be setting aside in your debt settlement war chest each month.

In our example, Mike owes $2,500 on his line of credit B, which has a $10,000 limit. Mike would like to keep this line of credit. This *means that Mike will be employing the Silverthorn Lite debt settlement strategy on $32,500 worth of debt instead of $35,000 as set out previously. Mike needs to save 50 per cent of $32,500, or $16,250. Mike wants to pay $150 a month on line of credit B. This means that instead of having $725 available each month to contribute to his debt settlement war chest, Mike now has only $575. If Mike contributes $575 a month into a dedicated debt settlement war chest bank account, it will take him about 29 months to save $16,250.*

Mike's plan for dealing with his $40,000 in debt is summarized in Figure 8. Mike will not be using the Silverthorn Lite debt settlement strategy on two of his debts, the $5,000 income debt owing to Canada Revenue Agency and the $2,500 owing on his line of credit B.

Figure 8: Mike's plan for eliminating $40,000 in unsecured debt

Debt	Amount	Money Set Aside for This Debt Each Month
Debts resolved using Silverthorn Lite debt settlement strategy		$575 for all debts included in Silverthorn Lite
Credit card A	$10,000	
Credit card B	$7,500	
Credit card C	$2,500	
Line of credit A	$7,500	
Loan	$5,000	
Subtotal	$32,500	
OTHER DEBTS		
Income Tax	$5,000	$275
Line of credit B	$2,500	$150
Subtotal	$7,500	
Total	$40,000	$1,000

3. Make any necessary banking arrangements.

In our example Mike is going to stop making payments on some credit cards, lines of credit, and a personal loan. If he obtained any of these products through a financial institution where he also has a chequing account or a savings account, he should anticipate that the financial institution, under a right of set-off, will seize money from these bank accounts to pay his debt on his credit cards, lines of credit, and personal loan.

PRACTICAL TIP

If you are going to stop making payments on a credit card, personal loan, line of credit, or bank overdraft that you obtained through a financial institution, you should sever all your relationships with that financial institution. This might mean you will have to open a new bank account at a new financial institution.

You can have your paycheque or any pension cheques or social assistance payments deposited into a new bank account. In addition, any bills paid out of your former account should in the future be paid from your new account, including any current pre-authorized debits you have. You should transfer any other assets to the new financial institution.

4. Develop a plan for dealing with collection calls.

The Silverthorn Lite debt settlement strategy involves stopping payments to some of your creditors. As a result, you will receive collection calls from them for the first six months that your accounts are in default. At some point they will send your overdue account to a collection agency and then you will start receiving collection calls from collection agencies.

PRACTICAL TIP

You may want to take advantage of the advice in Part One of this book to stop, avoid, or discourage the collection calls.

STAGE TWO: STOP MAKING PAYMENT TO CREDITORS AND AMASS YOUR DEBT SETTLEMENT WAR CHEST

Once you have completed the Planning and Preparation stage of the Silverthorn Lite debt settlement strategy, you are ready to begin Stage Two. You need to do two things during Stage Two: stop making payments to your creditors and begin to amass the money for your debt settlement war chest.

IMPORTANT FACT

To successfully use the Silverthorn Lite debt settlement strategy, you must, over the next two to three years, be able to come up with an amount of money equal to approximately 30 to 40 per cent of your existing unsecured consumer debt. This is an attainable goal for most people because they have stopped making payments on a significant amount of their current debt.

You might have several sources of funds for your debt settlement war chest: (1) setting aside money each month from your paycheque, (2) refinancing an existing mortgage on your property, (3) selling one or more assets of significant value, (4) borrowing money from a traditional lender, friends, or family, or (5) receiving an inheritance or payment arising from a lawsuit or divorce settlement.

For most people, amassing a debt settlement war chest means setting aside a specific amount of money each month from their paycheque. Some people might have access to a significant amount of money from the sale of a home, cottage, or recreational vehicle; a sizable income tax refund; or proceeds from an insurance claim or work-related injury.

PRACTICAL TIP

Set up automatic monthly transfers into a bank account whose sole purpose is to hold the money you're saving for debt settlement payments: your debt settlement war chest.

If the source of your debt settlement war chest funds is your paycheque, as soon as you get paid you should transfer a specific amount of money into a dedicated bank account. Your goal should be to set aside a certain amount each month. You should not use this bank account for any purpose other than setting aside money to be used as lump sum settlements.

Ideally, you should automate this process so you never have access to this money. You are wasting your time using the Silverthorn Lite debt settlement strategy if you are unable to successfully save money in accordance with your plan.

If you are having problems setting aside funds for a debt settlement war chest, you might want to retain the services of a debt settlement firm that requires you to make regular contributions into its trust account using a pre-authorized debit plan. My law firm usually requires debt settlement clients to deposit money for future lump sum settlements into my firm's trust account through pre-authorized debit. It's essentially a forced savings program.

STAGE THREE: NEGOTIATE YOUR LUMP SUM SETTLEMENTS

As you build your debt settlement war chest, you won't make any future payments to a creditor until it sends you a satisfactory written settlement offer. Then you can make a lump sum payment in accordance with the terms of the offer.

There is at least one major creditor who will negotiate generous lump settlements when accounts are in default for only six months. Therefore, depending on who your creditors are you might be negotiating a settlement as early as six months. However, if your goal is to obtain settlements in the 20- to 35-cent range or less, you will typically have to wait until your accounts have been in default for 24 to 36 months.

You will likely be conducting your settlement negotiations with a collector at a collection agency. This means you will want to avoid providing the collector with your phone number, otherwise you run the risk of being hounded by collectors. Ideally, you want to be in a position where a collector is unable to call you because you have an unlisted phone number and you can speak to the collector at times of your choosing.

PRACTICAL TIP
Consider getting an unlisted home phone number and dial *67 before you call the collection agency so your phone number is blocked.

You might feel uncomfortable negotiating your settlement with a collector at a collection agency. That isn't a problem. You can hire a debt settlement firm, a lawyer, or a paralegal to negotiate on your behalf. If they are experienced, they should be able to negotiate a generous settlement for you. The real question is how much these individuals will charge you for their assistance and what services they can offer you. Shop around before you hire someone to negotiate a debt settlement on your behalf.

As the amount of money in your debt settlement war chest increases, you will have more options about which settlements you can pursue. You might find it helpful to take the position that you are not going to consider any settlements below 25 cents on the dollar.

During Stage Three of the Silverthorn Lite debt settlement strategy, you might think of yourself as a bargain hunter shopping for great deals on eliminating your debt.

ADVANTAGES OF THE SILVERTHORN LITE DEBT SETTLEMENT STRATEGY
There are a number of reasons you might want to use this strategy to settle your debts:

1. You have the opportunity – results are not guaranteed – to settle some of your unsecured consumer liabilities for

approximately 20 to 35 cents on the dollar, and sometimes for even less.

2. It can provide you with immediate relief in your short-term cash flow situation.

3. It is a very flexible strategy, which means you can use it in conjunction with other options for resolving debts, including making instalment payments and taking advantage of the expiry of a limitation period to avoid paying a debt.

4. If things do not work out, you still have plenty of options, such as credit counselling, a consumer proposal, or personal bankruptcy.

DISADVANTAGES OF THE SILVERTHORN LITE DEBT SETTLEMENT STRATEGY

There are four negative consequences arising from using the Silverthorn Lite debt settlement strategy.

1. You will receive collection calls. In contrast, if you were to deal with your outstanding debts through credit counselling, a consumer proposal, or personal bankruptcy, you would not receive collection calls.

2. It will have a negative impact on your credit rating. Your debts will attain an R9 status until you settle them, when your credit report will be updated to show a zero balance.

3. The strategy can't be used for eliminating most debt owed to the government.

4. If you do not pay an overdue account, there is a risk you will be sued. But as noted earlier, when large creditors send their overdue accounts to a collection agency, it usually means the creditor has decided not to sue the consumer.

Even if your creditor *does* commence a lawsuit against you, you will still have an opportunity to prevent your creditor from obtaining a judgment against you. You might be able to pay the creditor's claim in full. In many cases, a creditor who sues you will be prepared to negotiate a settlement within a few days after commencing a lawsuit against you, for instance a lump sum payment of 80 per cent on the dollar payable within 30 days.

IMPORTANT FACT
It may be possible to negotiate a settlement for less than 100 cents on the dollar after you have been sued by your creditor.

One day I received a call from a man who was being sued for $13,000. He hired me to contact the creditor's lawyer and attempt to negotiate a settlement. I phoned the creditor's lawyer and he agreed not to take any action that would lead to obtaining a default judgment against my client without first giving me two weeks' notice. I offered to settle the lawsuit for a lump sum payment of $10,000, payable within 30 days. My client wanted to avoid having a wage garnishment and he arranged a second mortgage on his home. The creditor accepted the offer, my client successfully borrowed the $10,000, and the lawsuit was settled without my client's employer learning he had been sued.

The fact that the Silverthorn Lite debt settlement strategy involves the risk of being sued means that the strategy should be most attractive to the residents of Ontario, Alberta, Saskatchewan, and Quebec, where the statute of limitations on consumer debt is only two or three years. If you live in one of these four provinces, your potential exposure to being sued and paying pre-judgment and post-judgment interest is only two or three years, whereas it can potentially be six years in the rest of Canada.

DO-IT-YOURSELF VERSUS USING AN AGENT
You can follow the Silverthorn Lite debt settlement strategy yourself. You also have the option of using the services of a lawyer, paralegal, or debt settlement firm to assist you with it. A handful of firms in Canada today provide debt settlement services to

consumers, but in many cases, there may be nothing these firms can do for you that you could not do for yourself. They should, however, have some experience dealing with creditors and the manner in which they settle accounts that could be very helpful to you.

The firms providing debt settlement services often do little, if anything, to assist their clients with stopping, discouraging, or avoiding collection calls. Furthermore, these debt settlement companies may not assist their clients with setting aside money for their debt settlement war chest. Furthermore, these debt settlement companies may not assist their clients if they are sued. Finally, an employee working at a debt settlement company is not required to have any formal education, work experience, or professional designation. All they need is a pulse.

CHAPTER 17

THE SILVERTHORN MAX DEBT SETTLEMENT STRATEGY

In Chapter 16 we learned how, using the Silverthorn Lite debt settlement strategy, you can eliminate your unsecured consumer debts for 20 to 35 cents on the dollar, and sometimes less, by (1) ceasing to make payments to your creditors, (2) amassing a debt settlement war chest, and (3) over the next several years negotiating lump settlements with your creditors.

The Silverthorn Lite debt settlement strategy is an attractive option for anyone experiencing difficulties making the minimum payments on their credit cards or lines of credit, or anyone who owes more than $10,000 in consumer debt.

IMPORTANT FACT

The Silverthorn Lite debt settlement strategy explained in Chapter 16 assumes that you will be able to borrow or save money to settle your debts. You can use the Silverthorn Max strategy whether or not you are in a financial position to amass a debt settlement war chest.

The Silverthorn Max debt settlement strategy is a variation of the Silverthorn Lite strategy. It can assist you in dealing with your debts by taking maximum advantage of limitation periods. It should be particularly attractive to individuals who are unable to borrow money at a reasonable interest rate to deal with their current debt or those who cannot afford the added burden of borrowing money at high interest rates. The key difference between the two is that under Silverthorn Max, you wait for limitation periods to expire before you even consider doing any settlements.

Under the Silverthorn Max debt settlement strategy, you (1) stop making payments to certain unsecured consumer creditors, (2) wait for the relevant limitation periods to expire, (3) amass a debt settlement war chest *if you are in a financial position to do so,* and (4) once the limitation periods have expired, decide if you want to decline to pay any of your debts, *in which case you will have avoided paying any money to your creditors,* or you can attempt to negotiate very generous settlements with your unsecured creditors.

As long as you are not successfully sued before the relevant limitation period expires, you should be able to deal with your debt more cheaply than with any other option. Even if you *are* sued before the limitation periods expire, you might obtain favourable results, as you will see later in this chapter.

If you use the Silverthorn Max debt settlement strategy, no creditor successfully sues you, and you decide not to pay them, you will, with some exceptions, obtain all the advantages of filing for personal bankruptcy without any of the disadvantages.

At the end of this chapter we will review those circumstances where Silverthorn Max is both the *most attractive* and *least attractive* options for you. But first let me explain how it works.

HOW DOES THE SILVERTHORN MAX DEBT SETTLEMENT STRATEGY WORK?

The following four examples, two involving a person with the ability to amass a debt settlement war chest, and two in which a person has difficulty simply meeting day-to-day living expenses, will help illustrate the advantages of the Silverthorn Max debt settlement strategy.

Example A: Alberta resident named Sam is able to save up settlement money

Sam, 35 years old, single, living in Calgary, owes $50,000 in unsecured consumer debt and he is finding it virtually impossible to make the minimum monthly payments. He earns $55,000 a year working in the IT department at the head office of a large oil company doing tech support. He owns a condominium worth $200,000 and he owes $190,000 on his mortgage. Here is a list of Sam's unsecured debts.

Credit card A	*$10,000*
Credit card B	*$5,000*
Credit card C	*$5,000*
Credit card D	*$5,000*
Credit card E	*$5,000*
Credit card F	*$2,500*
Line of credit	*$7,500*
Personal loan	*$10,000*
Total	*$50,000*

Sam is currently making monthly payments totalling $1,500 to service this debt load. He recently had some major car expenses and consequently he doesn't think he'll be able to make the minimum payment on at least one of his credit cards this month.

If Sam were to employ the Silverthorn Max debt settlement strategy, he would stop making payments to all of these creditors after he takes necessary precautions to avoid having any money seized by his current financial institutions under the right of set-off. Sam opens two new bank accounts at his new financial institution, one for his personal banking needs, and a second account, his dedicated account for amassing his debt settlement war chest.

His goal is to save $25,000, 50 per cent of the $50,000 that he currently owes to his unsecured creditors. Sam is going to deposit $1,000 a month into this new bank account, an amount that is significantly less than the $1,500 he was previously paying to service his $50,000 debt load. Sam anticipates that he will be able to save the $25,000 over the next 25 months.

Sam stops making payments on all his unsecured debts. He gets an unlisted phone number. Seven months later, he starts getting phone calls at work from two collection agencies. Sam hires a lawyer to send these two collection agencies a cease and desist letter, advising them that the lawyer is representing Sam and that all future communications on his account are to be made to the lawyer's office – and not to anyone else! Twelve months later Sam receives calls from two different collection agencies after his accounts have been recalled by his creditor and then placed with new agencies. Sam pays a lawyer to send a cease and desist letter to these two new collection agencies.

Two years go by from the date of Sam's last payment on these accounts and Sam has not been sued on any of them. Sam can now choose not to pay any of these accounts because Alberta's two-year statute of limitations has expired on all these debts.

Sam decides not to pay any of these debts at the present time. If he chooses not to resolve these debts through settlement, he will avoid paying $50,000 in debt, plus any interest owing. However, he will have numerous R9s on his credit report for the next four years. Sam decides to wait another year, until these outstanding accounts are 36 months in default. Once his accounts have been in default for 36 months, Sam contacts the collection agencies representing all of his creditors to see what kind of settlements are available.

When Sam's outstanding accounts were first placed in collections, he learned that his creditors froze the interest owing on six of his eight debts once the debts were six months in default. This means that Sam is being charged interest for the entire 36 months on only two of his eight outstanding accounts. Sam learns that the outstanding balance on his original $50,000 debt, 36 months later, is now $60,000 and *that he can settle these eight debts totalling $60,000 for $15,000, or 25 cents on the dollar. Sam now has two options:*

Option A: Rely on the expiry of a limitation period

If Sam chooses to rely on the expiry of a limitation period he can avoid paying $60,000 to these creditors. If he does, these eight outstanding accounts will show up on his credit report for the next three years, at which time they will drop off. Sam will find it difficult to borrow money during this time.

Option B: Settle all his outstanding accounts for a total of $15,000

Sam can choose to settle these accounts for $15,000, in which case his credit report will be updated to show that these accounts are settled in full and they all have a zero balance. Sam should find it much easier to borrow money in the next three years if he settles these debts.

If you use the Silverthorn Max debt settlement strategy, as long as you are not sued before the expiry of a limitation period, you are in an excellent position to deal with your outstanding debts. You will have the option of not paying these creditors any money whatsoever or you can attempt to negotiate settlements with each of your creditors under the most generous possible terms.

In Example A Sam is not sued by a single creditor. Let's change the facts slightly. After Sam's $7,500 personal loan is 20 months in default, Sam is sued for $9,000, the principal of $7,500, as well as $1,500 in outstanding interest and court costs.

Example B: Sam is sued by one creditor for $9,000

Starting the first month Sam stopped making payments to his creditors, and each month thereafter, Sam deposited $1,000 into the bank account dedicated to amassing his debt settlement war chest. In month 20, he is sued for $9,000 on his outstanding loan. By now Sam has $20,000 in his war chest.

As soon as Sam is sued, he can make a settlement offer to the creditor suing him. He can do this himself or he can hire a lawyer or a paralegal to do it on his behalf. If he is sued for $9,000 it should be *possible to settle this lawsuit on the basis of a lump sum payment of approximately $7,500 or $8,000, payable within 30 days. Sam's creditor agrees to settle this lawsuit for $7,500 and Sam pays his lawyer $750 to negotiate the settlement, so his total cost to eliminate this personal loan is $8,250.*

In Example A, the total cost of settling all of Sam's $50,000 in debts was $15,000, of which let's say $2,250 was for the personal loan. In Example B, the cost of resolving the personal loan lawsuit is $8,250. This means that in Example B if Sam were to settle his other debts, his total cost for eliminating his $50,000 in debts is $21,000. The fact that Sam was sued for $9,000 increased his total cost of eliminating his debt through settlements by $6,000, from $15,000 to $21,000.

Example C: Ontario resident named Veronica is unable to save up settlement money

Veronica, age 45, recently separated, with two teenage daughters, lives in Toronto. She does not receive any child support or spousal support from her husband. She works full-time as an office manager in a dental office, earning $52,000 a year, but has no benefits, no pension plan, and no sick days. Veronica has 20 years' experience at the dental office and knows at least 20 dentists who would hire her if she were ever looking for a job. Veronica rents a three-bedroom townhouse and has no significant assets.

Veronica and her husband owe a total of $20,000 on some personal loans. For several years Veronica and her husband had four credit cards in both their names on which they carried small balances. In the last few months, however, Veronica's husband ran up tens of thousands of dollars in debt on these joint credit cards. This contributed to Veronica demanding that her husband move out, which he did two months ago. Veronica has learned that her husband filed for personal bankruptcy last month, which means that he is no longer legally responsible to pay for any of this debt on their joint credit cards. However, she is still responsible for the debts. For the past two months

Veronica has made the minimum payments on these credit cards but she can no longer afford to do so. Today Veronica has $100,000 in debt as summarized below:

Credit card A	*$30,000*
Credit card B	*$20,000*
Credit card C	*$15,000*
Credit card D	*$10,000*
Personal loan X	*$10,000*
Personal loan Y	*$10,000*
Line of credit	*$5,000*
Total	*$100,000*

If Veronica were to employ the Silverthorn Max debt settlement strategy, she would not make any payments on any of these debts. She is not in a position to set aside any money to amass a debt settlement war chest. She does open a new bank account at a new financial institution.

Veronica is not sued on a single account within the 24-month period after the date of her last payment. By the time these accounts are 36 months in default, Veronica has no money available to use negotiating lump sum settlements. Since Veronica was not sued by a single one of her creditors, she can avoid paying all these accounts. In the event she were ever sued by any of these creditors, it would be important for her to file a defence pleading the expiry of Ontario's two-year statute of limitations as a complete defence to the creditor's claim.

Let's change the facts in Example C so that Veronica's three largest creditors sue her for $70,000.

Example D: Veronica is sued for $70,000
Veronica's three largest creditors sue her for a total of $70,000, and within a few months they obtain judgments against her. She has no money available to settle these lawsuits. Are the creditors ever going

to recover any money from her? There is a good chance they will never recover a penny!

Veronica does not own a house, so her creditors might never be in a position to recover money from her by using a writ of execution and obtaining a lien on real estate. Her creditors might never be able to seize money from Veronica's bank accounts, and she could arrange her finances so that in the future she doesn't even have a bank account! Alternatively, she might open a new bank account or a joint account with one of her teenage daughters for her personal banking needs, or she might maintain a bank account in her own name but keep as little money as possible in it at any point in time.

Veronica's creditors will probably want to recover money from her using a wage garnishment. Under the Ontario Wages Act, the maximum amount of Veronica's wages that can be seized through wage garnishment is 20 per cent of her take-home pay. If Veronica's monthly take-home pay were $2,855.02, the most that could be seized under a wage garnishment is $571 a month.

But these three creditors might never be able to successfully obtain a nickel through a wage garnishment, because in order to obtain a garnishment order, they need to know the name and address of her employer. If Veronica learns that her employer has received a garnishment order, she can simply quit her job and get another one as an office manager at one of Toronto's several hundred other dental offices. She can simply ask the receptionist at her new employer not to disclose her name to anyone calling the dental office. By quitting her job, Veronica has effectively defeated the garnishment order.

In this example, where Veronica uses the Silverthorn Max debt settlement strategy, she might never have to pay a nickel of her outstanding debt, even though she is sued for $70,000. In addition, Veronica is able to take advantage of Silverthorn Max despite the fact that she was never able to set aside money that could be used to negotiate settlements with her creditors.

ADVANTAGES OF USING THE SILVERTHORN MAX DEBT SETTLEMENT STRATEGY

There are a number of advantages to using Silverthorn Max to resolve your debts:

1. It is a very flexible strategy. Unlike credit counselling, a consumer proposal, and personal bankruptcy, you can choose which debts you use it for, rather than including all of them. You may want to pay a debt owed to the government in full or in instalments. You may want to do the same with a debt owing to your employer or a family member or on a debt where a family member acted as a guarantor.

2. You have the potential to avoid paying one or more of your debts altogether. You may be overwhelmed with a significant amount of debt. You may be considering making a consumer proposal or filing for personal bankruptcy. This may not be necessary or in your best interests if your creditors do not sue you. Even if you are sued, there is no guarantee that your creditors will recover any money from you. If your creditors do obtain judgments against you, depending on which province you live in, you might be in a position to go to court and reduce your liability on the basis of financial hardship.

PRACTICAL TIP
If you are contemplating credit counselling, a consumer proposal, or personal bankruptcy, you might want to consider trying the Silverthorn Max debt settlement strategy first. If you are unable to successfully resolve your debt situation this way, you can always try the other options.

3. You have the potential to eliminate your existing unsecured consumer debt for approximately 20 to 35 cents on the dollar, or sometimes even less, over the next 36 months.

DISADVANTAGES OF USING THE SILVERTHORN MAX DEBT SETTLEMENT STRATEGY

A person employing the Silverthorn Max debt settlement strategy will face the same disadvantages as the person using Silverthorn Lite: you will receive collection calls, you might be sued, and it will have a negative impact on your credit rating. You might want to avoid using the Silverthorn Max debt settlement strategy if it is crucial that you be able to borrow large sums of money in the next few years at the lowest available interest rates. In addition, Silverthorn Max is not available to eliminate government debt, except for provincial student loans and Canada Student Loans obtained from a Canadian chartered bank between August 1, 1995, and July 31, 2000.

If you are going to successfully use the Silverthorn Max debt settlement strategy, it will help if you are a risk-taker. Results are not guaranteed.

The Silverthorn Max debt settlement strategy may not be suitable for you if

1. you are unable to cope with collection calls or to devise a plan to deal with collection calls,
2. you are not prepared to assume the risk of being sued,
3. you are in a financial position where you can eliminate your debt using a debt consolidation loan at a rate of interest below 8 per cent, provided you can afford the additional debt burden, or
4. you are in a financial position where you can eliminate your debt using instalment payments over the next 6 to 18 months.

PERSONS FOR WHOM SILVERTHORN MAX MIGHT BE AN IDEAL SOLUTION

Certain people might find the Silverthorn Max debt settlement strategy most useful.

1. Residents of Ontario, Quebec, Alberta and Saskatchewan

The statute of limitations is only two years for residents of Ontario, Alberta, and Saskatchewan, and only three years in Quebec. If you live in one of these four provinces, your creditors have a relatively short window of time in which to sue you. The expiry of a limitation period is a "get out of jail free card," so from a debtor's perspective, the shorter the limitation period the better.

2. Individuals whose legal responsibility to pay a debt will expire in less than three years

You might not live in Ontario, Alberta, Saskatchewan, or Quebec but your debts have been in default for more than three years. This means that the limitation period on your debt is fast approaching and you will not have to pay your unsecured consumer debt if you are not sued before it expires.

3. Those who do not own any real estate

If you don't own any real estate and a creditor sues you, it will be limited to doing a wage garnishment. In many provinces, there are limits on how much of a person's pay is subject to wage garnishments. In Ontario, for example, 80 per cent of a person's take-home pay is exempt.

4. Those with no government debt or relatively little government debt

You cannot use the Silverthorn Max debt settlement strategy to avoid legal liability to pay a government debt. However, you will be successful employing the Silverthorn Max debt settlement strategy if you do not make payments on a government debt and the government does not successfully sue you.

5. Those who have previously filed for personal bankruptcy

Bankruptcy laws in Canada today are punitive toward those who have already filed for personal bankruptcy.

6. Those for whom personal bankruptcy is unattractive

If personal bankruptcy is very unattractive to you, for any reason, you might want to try the Silverthorn Max debt settlement strategy.

7. Individuals who are judgment proof or borderline "judgment proof"

If you are "judgment proof," you might find it very attractive to use the Silverthorn Max debt settlement strategy. To learn more about whether you are judgment proof, see Chapter 9, "Your Creditor Will Be Unable to Enforce a Judgment Against You.".

In Example D we saw how Veronica might avoid paying a penny even though three creditors obtained a judgment against her. I would not describe Veronica as judgment proof but as *borderline judgment proof* because she can probably avoid wage garnishments by changing jobs. Accordingly, if you are borderline judgment proof like Veronica you might want to consider using the Silverthorn Max debt settlement strategy.

CHAPTER 18

DEBT MANAGEMENT PLAN WITH A CREDIT COUNSELLING AGENCY

You might be able to afford to repay your debts in full if you were given several years to do so. That's just what a debt management plan is for: it allows you to eliminate your unsecured consumer debts in monthly payments over a period of up to five years. You can arrange for one through a credit counselling agency, and many Canadians do so in an attempt to avoid personal bankruptcy.

THE TWO TYPES OF CREDIT COUNSELLING AGENCIES

Most Canadians do not know much about credit counselling except that it might be a good idea to "go for credit counselling" when you are in financial trouble. There are two different types of credit counselling agencies in Canada, non-profits and for-profits.

IMPORTANT FACT

If you decide to repay your debt under a debt management plan, you should be able to do so at a lower cost through a non-profit credit counselling agency than a for-profit one.

If you decide to take advantage of a debt management plan, and you are at the point of choosing a credit counselling agency, you should understand some of the differences between a non-profit and for-profit credit counselling agency, and you should know whether a specific agency you are contemplating enrolling with is a non-profit or a for-profit.

Credit counselling agencies charge a fee for their services, a percentage of the total debt included in your debt management plan. In most cases, you will pay this fee when you make a payment. For example, if your monthly payments to your creditors under your plan are $100 a month and you are charged fees of 10 per cent, your fee is $10 per month. Some for-profit credit counselling agencies might front-load this fee, in which case you could be paying thousands of dollars to the credit counselling agency before a nickel is paid to your creditors.

IMPORTANT FACT

The majority of front-line counsellors working at credit counselling agencies will not act zealously in your best interests and provide you with all your options for dealing with your debt situation. In Part Three of this book I explained several reasons you might never have to pay your outstanding account – a credit counsellor is unlikely to give you this information.

It will cost you more to enroll in a debt management plan with a for-profit credit counselling agency than with a non-profit credit one. For-profits typically charge their clients fees equal to 15 per cent of the amount of debt included in a plan, whereas many non-profits charge their clients fees of about 10 per cent. In some cases, a non-profit credit counselling agency may even waive fees altogether or simply request that you make a donation to their agency. Non-profit credit counselling agencies are able to do this because they collect money on behalf of Canada's chartered banks and other major creditors and are compensated generously by them for doing so.

When you enroll in a debt management plan with a *non-profit* credit counselling agency, you are entitled to significant interest relief on your outstanding balance. And if you owe money to a bank you will typically not pay *any* interest on your outstanding balance. You will forfeit this interest relief if you fail to successfully complete your debt management plan. When you enroll in a debt management plan with a *for-profit* credit counselling agency you will not be entitled to any interest relief.

IMPORTANT FACT

If you decide to repay your debts using a debt management plan, I would not recommend that you do so through a for-profit credit counselling agency, because (1) you will likely not be entitled to any interest relief on your outstanding balance during the life of your plan, and (2) the fees you pay to a for-profit credit counselling agency will likely be higher than the fees you would pay to a non-profit one.

WHAT HAPPENS AFTER YOU ENROLL IN A DEBT MANAGEMENT PLAN

After you have enrolled in a debt management plan, your credit counselling agency will contact your creditors and advise them that you have done so. Your credit counselling agency will potentially discuss three issues with each of your creditors:

1. The threshold issue of whether the creditor will permit you to repay your debt over a period of time under a debt management plan
2. The terms of your repayment of principal, or the debt itself
3. The terms of any relief on interest being charged on your outstanding balance during the life of your plan

If you owe money to the government, it will not agree to have you pay your debt under a debt management plan. Where your creditor has obtained a judgment against you and your paycheque is subject to a wage garnishment, your creditor is unlikely to agree to the plan. In addition, a creditor that has commenced a lawsuit against you or one that is about to might decline to participate.

Furthermore, one or more of your creditors might refuse to permit you to repay a specific debt over a period of time if they feel you are in a financial position to pay it right now. I know a woman who enrolled in credit counselling and a bank refused to agree to the debt management plan because she had significant equity in her home; it wanted her to borrow money to pay off the debt using her home as collateral.

Assuming your creditor agrees that your debt can be included in the plan, your credit counselling agency and your creditor will negotiate the number of months during which you will make payments, as well as the interest payable. Your credit counselling agency will know, given your particular financial situation, the total amount of money you have available each month to pay your creditors. Each of them would prefer that you repay your debt as quickly as possible under your plan, but your credit counselling agency should negotiate a plan that you can afford.

Your credit counselling agency will then arrange for you to make regular payments to it, usually weekly, bi-weekly, or monthly. Your agency will in turn forward money to your creditors.

PRACTICAL TIP
Never enroll in a debt management plan if the fees are front-loaded. If you do, you could be paying thousands of dollars in fees to a credit counselling agency before you even make your first payment to your creditors.

Your enrollment in a debt management plan will have a number of consequences, some positive and some negative. On the positive side, collection calls should cease as soon as the collection agencies are advised that you have entered into credit counselling. Both your unsecured creditors and their collection agents should not engage in any additional collection activity on an account included in your debt management plan. If, however, you owe money to the government, the fact that you have entered credit counselling will not stop collection calls on those debts.

Your enrollment in a debt management plan will not affect any existing wage garnishments. Once your debt is included in a debt management plan, your creditor will list your account on your credit report as an R7. You will not be able to borrow money during the life of the plan.

You will continue to make payments under your debt management plan until the total amount owing to your creditors is paid in full. If you fail to make your payments, you will no longer be entitled to interest relief, and all the interest you would otherwise have avoided paying will be added back on to your balance owing.

ADVANTAGES OF A DEBT MANAGEMENT PLAN

1. You obtain immediate relief by reducing the amount of your monthly payments to your unsecured consumer creditors.
2. You will no longer receive collection calls on your unsecured consumer debts.
3. You reduce the risk of being sued.

DISADVANTAGES OF A DEBT MANAGEMENT PLAN

1. It is not a cost-effective manner in which to eliminate debt. Under a debt management plan you will be paying your creditors 100 per cent of the outstanding principal and interest owing as of the date you enroll in the plan. You will also be required to pay fees of 10 to 15 per cent to your credit counselling agency.

The total cost of eliminating your debt under a debt management plan arranged through a non-profit credit counselling agency should be somewhere between 100 cents and 115 cents on the dollar. The cost of eliminating your debt through a for-profit agency could be anywhere between 125 cents and 130 cents on the dollar, depending on the average rate of interest charged on your outstanding balance.

2. You will be required to include *all* your debts in a debt management plan – even those you could avoid paying because the relevant limitation period has expired.

3. You cannot settle your debts for less than 100 cents on the dollar.

4. It will have a negative impact on your credit rating.

WHEN A DEBT MANAGEMENT PLAN IS AN IDEAL SOLUTION

There are three situations in which a debt management plan might be an ideal option.

1. To buy you some time before you file for personal bankruptcy, if you have outstanding student loans. When you file for personal bankruptcy you are relieved of your obligation to repay your unsecured debts, except outstanding student loans – unless you ceased to be a full-time student more than seven years before your bankruptcy.

PRACTICAL TIP

If you owe significant money in student loans and you want to file for bankruptcy, you may want to use a debt management plan until seven years has passed since you were a full-time student. At that point, you will not be legally responsible to pay your student loan debt after your bankruptcy.

Mohamed owes $60,000 in student loans and he ceased attending school five years ago. If Mohamed were to file for personal bankruptcy today, his $60,000 student loan debt would survive bankruptcy. Ideally, Mohamed should file for personal bankruptcy after he has ceased to be a full-time student for a minimum of seven years. Mohamed can enter a debt management plan anticipating that he will drop out of his plan once he has ceased to be a full-time student for seven years.

IMPORTANT FACT

Be aware that if you advise a credit counsellor that you intend to drop out of a debt management plan before its completion, the agency may decline to act on your behalf.

2. You are seeking protection from your creditors and you anticipate that your financial situation will improve in the future. You might want to enter into a debt management plan for 24 to 36 months, or in some cases longer, in order to get temporary protection from your creditors. During this period you will not be receiving collection calls on any unsecured consumer debts included in your debt management plan, nor should you be sued on these debts. This strategy is most attractive if you do not have a significant amount of debt.

3. You owe less than $10,000 and you are not a suitable candidate for debt settlement. In some situations, you might be an ideal candidate for credit counselling where debt settlement, a consumer proposal, or personal bankruptcy (more on these latter two in the next chapter) are not attractive options for you. A consumer proposal is not a viable option if you owe less than $10,000, and possibly less than $20,000, in debt. Debt settlement is not suitable for people who are uncomfortable with the risk of potential lawsuits and of dealing with collection calls.

4. You owe less than $30,000 in debt and you do not want to do a consumer proposal or file for personal bankruptcy. It seems a shame to file for personal bankruptcy if you are less than $30,000 in debt. If you owe $30,000 in debt and you make a consumer proposal, and your payments become three months in arrears, you will likely end up filing for personal bankruptcy. Therefore, if you owe less than $30,000 you might want to consider credit counselling, particularly if debt settlement is not an attractive option for you.

CHAPTER 19

CONSUMER PROPOSAL AND PERSONAL BANKRUPTCY

Every day, I speak on the phone with individuals who are experiencing major debt challenges. Recently, I had a conversation with Brenda (not her real name), whose husband had just moved out, leaving her with sole custody of their two young children in the family home. Before the separation, Brenda worked part-time as a dental hygienist and her husband worked at an auto-parts plant. He helped out with their kids' child care. The money Brenda currently receives from her husband is substantially less than he contributed toward household expenses before they separated.

Now that Brenda's husband has moved out, she has to pay more for child care expenses. To make matters worse, he has received a layoff notice. Brenda currently works 24 hours per week, and she has been told that her hours may be cut to 16 hours a week in the near future. Brenda is facing a significant reduction in net household income, even if she finds full-time employment at another dental office – a tall order for someone raising two young children on her own.

When you are facing serious debt problems like Brenda's, seeing a bankruptcy trustee may be your last resort. A bankruptcy trustee can assist you with two of your eight options for dealing with your debt situation: making a consumer proposal and filing for personal bankruptcy. Ideally, you will see a bankruptcy trustee only when none of the other six options for dealing with your debt have worked or make sense in your situation. Most people who make a consumer proposal or file for personal bankruptcy are facing a major interruption in income – individuals who have lost their job or whose marriage or common-law relationship has ended.

PRACTICAL TIP

If your objective is to make a consumer proposal or file for personal bankruptcy it will be necessary for you to meet in person with a bankruptcy trustee. You can find a trustee by looking in the Yellow Pages or on the Internet.

A WORD ABOUT BANKRUPTCY TRUSTEES

A bankruptcy trustee is someone who has a significant amount of educational training and practical experience. Most trustees have a background in accounting, and many even have an accounting designation, such as a Chartered Accountant or a Chartered General Accountant. Before an individual receives her trustee's licence from the Office of the Superintendent of Bankruptcy, a division of the federal government, she must pass a series of courses and examinations, culminating in a final written exam and then a final oral examination. On average it takes at least five years to obtain a trustee's licence after getting an accounting designation, so the process is long and difficult, which is why there are fewer than 900 licensed trustees in Canada.

Many Canadians mistakenly believe that a bankruptcy trustee works for a bank. In fact, bankruptcy trustees are independent. The bankruptcy trustee is not your advocate – her role is not to get you the best possible outcome at the expense of your creditors. A bankruptcy trustee has obligations under the federal Bankruptcy

& Insolvency Act to the Superintendent of Bankruptcy, to your creditors, and to you. If you file for personal bankruptcy or make a consumer proposal, in many respects the bankruptcy trustee acts like a judge at a trial in which the debtor is one party and the other party is his creditors.

IMPORTANT FACT

You should not expect a bankruptcy trustee to review your entire financial situation and to advise you on which course of action to take.

Bankruptcy trustees receive financial compensation from the consumers who deal with them. You will pay the trustee approximately $1,600 to $1,700 to file for personal bankruptcy. You do not directly pay the bankruptcy trustee to make a consumer proposal; her fees come out of your contributions. If you make an appointment to see a bankruptcy trustee and you do not subsequently make a consumer proposal or file for personal bankruptcy, the bankruptcy trustee will not receive a penny in financial compensation.

INSOLVENCY REQUIREMENT

IMPORTANT FACT

To make a consumer proposal or to file for personal bankruptcy, you must be *insolvent*. You are insolvent if (1) the total dollar value of your debts is greater than the total dollar value of your assets, *and* (2) you are unable to pay your financial obligations as they become due.

Many people who are experiencing significant financial problems are not insolvent, and therefore neither a consumer proposal nor personal bankruptcy is available to them as an option for dealing with their debts *at the present time*. The following example illustrates this point.

Mike recently lost his job. He has had no income for the past four months and is unable to pay his property taxes and utilities. Today Mike owes $75,000 to his creditors. Mike's only asset in the world is his townhouse, which has a market value of $200,000 with no mortgage.

In this example Mike is not insolvent because he meets only one of the two requirements of insolvency: he cannot pay his financial obligations as they become due. The total dollar value of Mike's debts, $75,000, does not exceed the dollar value of his assets, $200,000. Mike could sell his townhouse for $200,000 and use the sale proceeds to pay off the $75,000 owing to his creditors.

WHAT YOU SHOULD KNOW BEFORE YOU SEE A BANKRUPTCY TRUSTEE

Before you make an appointment to see a bankruptcy trustee it is very important that you have a thorough understanding of *all your options* for dealing with your particular debt situation. You owe it to yourself, and your family, to ensure that you have exhausted all other reasonable alternatives.

In particular, if you (1) live in a province where the statute of limitations is only two or three years – Ontario, Quebec, Alberta, or Saskatchewan – or (2) live anywhere else in Canada but the date of your last payment on the majority of your unsecured consumer debt is more than three years ago, it might be in your best interests to employ a wait-it-out strategy and see if the limitation period is going to expire. You might want to give serious consideration to postponing meeting with a bankruptcy trustee for two or three years. By doing so, you might be able to avoid paying some of your debts altogether.

IMPORTANT FACT

Bankruptcy trustees get paid when you make a consumer proposal or file for personal bankruptcy. They are unlikely to talk to you about any of the reasons that you might never have to pay a debt, which I outlined in Part Three.

INITIAL MEETING WITH A BANKRUPTCY TRUSTEE

At your initial meeting with a bankruptcy trustee, the trustee will want to determine if you are insolvent, and therefore eligible to make a consumer proposal or file for personal bankruptcy. He will want some information about the dollar value of both your assets and your debts. Either at this meeting or at a subsequent meeting, you will be asked to provide a list of all your creditors and the amounts owing to them. This list forms part of what is known as your *Statement of Affairs.*

It is important for you to list all your creditors in your Statement of Affairs because if a creditor is not listed, it will not receive the notice of your filing, and it may continue to attempt to recover money from you.

Note that the date of last payment on an outstanding debt is not recorded on a Statement of Affairs, nor is it common practice among bankruptcy trustees in Canada to find out the date of last payment. If a bankruptcy trustee does not make inquiries about the date of last payment on your debt it would make it virtually impossible for him to advise you if a limitation period had expired on your debt.

CONSUMER PROPOSAL

One of your eight options for dealing with your unsecured consumer debt is a consumer proposal. In a typical proposal a debtor makes payments to creditors of $200 to $1,000 a month for three to five years. The maximum period for a consumer proposal is five years. In most consumer proposals a debtor will repay approximately 30 per cent of all the monies owing to his unsecured creditors.

When is a consumer proposal available to you?
There are three things that will prevent you from resolving your debt situation using a consumer proposal: failing to satisfy the insolvency test, owing too much money to your creditors, or owing less than $10,000 to your creditors.

1. You must be insolvent. As noted earlier, you are not eligible to make a consumer proposal unless you satisfy the two-part insolvency requirement.

2. Your total debts cannot exceed $250,000 (excluding the mortgage on your principal residence). This amount increases to $500,000 if you and your spouse do a joint filing for a consumer proposal. However, if you are insolvent and your debts do exceed this amount, you are eligible to do a Division I Proposal, which is similar in many respects to a consumer proposal.

3. Your unsecured debts cannot be less than $10,000. The bankruptcy trustee (referred to as the *proposal administrator* in a consumer proposal) charges creditors a base fee regardless of the amount of your debt, so there is a good chance that your creditors will not accept a consumer proposal if you owe less than $10,000 in unsecured debt.

How a consumer proposal is made
The consumer proposal is prepared after a detailed review of your financial situation, including income and expenses. You work with the trustee to determine how much money you can afford to pay your creditors each month. The trustee reviews your total indebtedness to your unsecured creditors and determines the number of months over which payments are to be made. After this proposal is completed, it is filed with the Office of the Superintendent of Bankruptcy.

IMPORTANT FACT

On the date that your bankruptcy trustee files your consumer proposal with the Office of the Superintendent of Bankruptcy, all civil legal proceedings are *stayed* or suspended against you, except for garnishments for child support and spousal support.

A consumer proposal must be approved by a simple majority of your unsecured creditors, and each creditor is entitled to one vote for each dollar owing to it. This means that the power to approve or reject your consumer proposal can rest with just one or two of your largest unsecured creditors. Most consumer proposals are rejected unless you offer to pay all your unsecured creditors at least 30 per cent of the debt owed over a period not to exceed five years, although in some circumstances proposals may be accepted or rejected for amounts higher or lower than 30 per cent.

Each creditor reacts differently to a consumer proposal, so it is to your advantage to use a proposal administrator who has a significant amount of experience doing consumer proposals. For example, some banks have a policy requiring a minimum of 30 cents on the dollar on a consumer proposal. Some banks, however, will accept less than 30 cents on the dollar. It is critical that your trustee review your list of creditors so you can get informed advice about which offer is likely to be accepted by your creditors.

IMPORTANT FACT

Your creditors will typically accept or reject your consumer proposal within two months.

What happens if your creditors do not accept a consumer proposal?

If your consumer proposal is rejected by your creditors, you have three alternatives, two of which might still lead to the acceptance of a consumer proposal. First of all, you can ask your consumer proposal administrator to contact your creditors and ask them if they are willing to reconsider your proposal. It is possible that your creditors simply misunderstood your proposal. Second, your administrator can communicate with your creditors and find out what kind of consumer proposal would be acceptable to them. You would likely have to pay out more to your unsecured creditors than you would have under your original consumer proposal. If, for example, they didn't accept $200 a month over four years, they might be willing to accept $200 a month over five years.

Finally, another option is to file for personal bankruptcy if your financial situation has not improved and you can't settle your debts. Now that your consumer proposal has been rejected, about a couple of months have elapsed and your creditors will probably be much more aggressive about recovering money from you. If they sued you before you filed the consumer proposal, they will aggressively (1) seek a judgment against you, and (2) seek to enforce a judgment against you. Filing for bankruptcy will protect you from this.

IMPORTANT FACT
When your consumer proposal is rejected, any stay of civil legal proceedings against you is lifted.

What happens after a consumer proposal is accepted?
Under the typical consumer proposal, you make monthly payments directly to your proposal administrator, who then distributes the funds to your creditors. Occasionally it is possible to make a consumer proposal based upon a lump sum payment. A lump sum proposal might be an option if a spouse or family member gives you money, or if you sell an asset such as your home and use the sale proceeds for this purpose.

IMPORTANT FACT
It is very important that you not default on your monthly payment obligations under a consumer proposal.

A significant number of costs are associated with a consumer proposal, including these:

- Administrator's fees of $1,500, plus 20 per cent of all distributions
- Government filing fee of $100, plus a levy of 5 per cent on the amount of money included in your consumer proposal

You do not pay these fees on top of your monthly payment, so in effect your creditors absorb these fees.

If you become more than three months in arrears on your payments under a consumer proposal, it will be annulled and personal bankruptcy, while not automatic, may be inevitable. Basically, you will be back in the same position you were before starting your consumer proposal, except that you will get credit for any payments you made during the life of the consumer proposal. You will also have to pay interest on your outstanding balance. Some of your payments may have already been distributed to your creditors, but they may calculate interest from the start of the proposal, so if you default on it you will still have a significant level of debt.

IMPORTANT FACT

A significant number of people who successfully make a consumer proposal do not complete it, which typically means they end up filing for personal bankruptcy.

As many as one-quarter of individuals who make a consumer proposal do not successfully complete it. The most common reason for defaulting on monthly payment obligations is the loss of employment. A significant increase in a consumer's monthly living expenses might also cause her to default on her monthly payments, such as when she needs to buy a car or replace her existing one.

Advantages of a consumer proposal

There are a number of advantages to doing a consumer proposal. These can be summarized as follows:

1. You can eliminate your unsecured debt over a period, not to exceed five years, for approximately 30 cents on the dollar. The actual cost of a consumer proposal will depend on your assets, your income, the nature of your debts, and your ability to pay.

IMPORTANT FACT

The cost of eliminating your debt under a consumer proposal, typically around 30 cents on the dollar, will be significantly cheaper than a debt management plan arranged through a credit counselling agency, which will cost you somewhere between 100 and 120 cents on the dollar.

2. Collection calls will stop. As soon as your consumer proposal is filed with the Office of the Superintendent of Bankruptcy, it is illegal for your creditors and their collection agents to make collection calls to you. This is one reason you might choose a consumer proposal over a debt settlement strategy.

3. Interest will stop accruing on the outstanding balance. On the date your consumer proposal is filed with the Office of the Superintendent of Bankruptcy, interest on the unsecured debts listed in your Statement of Affairs will be frozen. This is another reason you might choose a consumer proposal over a debt settlement strategy.

4. You should be able to retain the equity in your home and retain your assets, including ownership in shares of a company. If you file for personal bankruptcy, you will likely lose the equity in your home, unless your province exempts a certain amount of equity in your principal residence from seizure.

5. You are not required to make surplus income payments, something you might be required to do if you file for personal bankruptcy, depending on your income and the number of your dependants. If you earn more than $30,000 or $40,000 a year, these surplus income payments could be costly to you.

Disadvantages of a consumer proposal

There are three disadvantages to doing a consumer proposal. If one or more of these disadvantages are important to you, you might want to consider either a debt settlement strategy or even credit counselling.

1. You aren't entitled to have credit during the period you are making payments under a consumer proposal. This means that a person who needs ready access to credit, such as a businessperson who travels frequently, might find a consumer proposal unattractive. It might also pose major headaches for a small business owner who is not incorporated, or for someone who needs to borrow money for a major purchase such as a car.

IMPORTANT FACT

A significant number of people who make a consumer proposal subsequently file for personal bankruptcy because of an unforeseen expense – for example, their car breaks down or they need to borrow money to obtain a car. You cannot borrow money as long as you are making payments to creditors under a consumer proposal.

PRACTICAL TIP

If you are going to make a consumer proposal and it is absolutely necessary for you to have an automobile, it might be prudent to lease or purchase one that should last you for the next five years. Once your consumer proposal is accepted, it will be very difficult to purchase or lease a car using credit for the next three to five years.

2. You must include all your unsecured debts in a consumer proposal. This might make it unattractive to you for one or more reasons:

- You will have to include debts in a consumer proposal even if the limitation period has expired.
- You will have to include a debt owing to your employer.
- You will have to include debts owing to friends or family members.
- You will have to include debts on which family members or friends are a guarantor.

In contrast, if you use debt settlement and/or the Silverthorn Lite or Max strategy, you will be able to pick and choose how to deal with a particular debt (although as usual your options for handling government debt will be limited). Depending on your particular financial situation, the fact that you must include all your unsecured debt in a consumer proposal can be a major disadvantage, as the following example illustrates.

Brian, an Ontario resident, sees a bankruptcy trustee and wants to discuss a consumer proposal. The bankruptcy trustee asks Brian to list all of his unsecured debt. They are as follows:

Loan from Brian's employer	*$10,000*
Bank personal loan	*$5,000*
Bank line of credit	*$5,000*
Sears credit card	*$15,000*
The Bay credit card	*$15,000*
Total	*$50,000*

Let's look at two different scenarios available to Brian: Scenario A, a consumer proposal under which Brian's creditors accept 30 cents on the dollar, and Scenario B, under which he doesn't make a consumer proposal but instead takes advantage of both limitation periods and debt settlement options.

Scenario A: Consumer proposal under which creditors accept 30 cents on the dollar

If Brian makes a consumer proposal, his employer will receive written notice from his proposal administrator. To add insult to injury, under the consumer proposal, Brian's employer will receive only $3,000 of the $10,000 owing to it. Could this affect Brian's Christmas bonus or his next raise? Brian is worried that he could lose his job or hurt his chance of advancement at his company if he does not repay his $10,000 loan in full. Furthermore, the date of Brian's last payment on his Sears and Bay credit cards is more than five years ago, which means those debts have expired under Ontario's two-year statute of limitations. Despite the fact that the limitation period has expired on $30,000 of Brian's $50,000 in unsecured debt, Brian has to include those two debts in his consumer proposal.

If Brian's creditors accept a consumer proposal at 30 cents on the dollar, Brian will have to pay his unsecured creditors $15,000 over a three- to five-year period. Furthermore, Brian will likely inform his employer that despite the fact that it will be receiving $3,000 from the bankruptcy trustee, Brian will voluntarily pay his employer $7,000 in connection with his employee loan. This means that the consumer proposal will actually cost Brian $22,000, and not $15,000. Brian will not be able to borrow any money for the period during which he is making payments under his consumer proposal – that is, for the next three to five years.

Scenario B: No consumer proposal

In contrast, Brian would be much better off not doing a consumer proposal. This would enable him to take advantage of the expiry of the limitation period on the two five-year-old credit card debts, reducing *his total liability from $50,000 to $20,000. Brian would have three options for dealing with the $10,000 he owes to the banks: (1) making instalment payments, which might cost him between $11,000 and $13,000, depending on the amount of interest he ultimately pays, (2) waiting for the expiry of Ontario's two-year limitation period, in which case he would have avoided paying the debt altogether, provided he were not sued during this 24-month period (and the odds of a chartered bank suing Brian for $5,000 are incredibly low), or (3) waiting 24 to 36 months and settling these two debts totalling $10,000 for lump sum payments of approximately $2,500, or 25 cents on the dollar. Brian could repay the entire $10,000 owing to his employer, and his employer would not receive a written notice from a bankruptcy trustee that Brian was making a consumer proposal to his creditors.*

Without making a consumer proposal, Brian will be able to deal with his debt situation for an amount between $10,000 and $23,000. Brian is not barred from obtaining credit if he chooses not to make a consumer proposal.

3. If you become three months in arrears making payments under a consumer proposal, it is annulled, which means that filing for personal bankruptcy is almost inevitable – although not automatic. In contrast, if you employ the Silverthorn Lite or Max debt settlement strategies and you cannot set aside any money for three months toward your settlement war chest, you will not face any negative consequences.

Persons for whom a consumer proposal is an ideal solution
A consumer proposal is a good solution for the following people:

1. People earning more than $30,000 or $40,000 a year. If this describes you and you file for bankruptcy, you will likely have to make surplus income payments to your bankruptcy trustee for 21 months, or longer for a second-time bankrupt. That is not the case with a consumer proposal.

2. People with significant equity in their homes. A bankrupt will typically lose his home if he has any equity in it, but in a consumer proposal he can keep his home.

3. People with assets worth a significant amount of money. In a bankruptcy any property that is non-exempt will be sold and the proceeds distributed to the bankrupt's creditors. In a consumer proposal, the debtor is entitled to keep all of his assets.

4. People who own shares in their own companies. In a bankruptcy a bankrupt might be required to sell the shares of his own companies, and the proceeds of the sale will be distributed to his creditors.

5. People with large student loans who have not ceased attending school at least seven years ago. A consumer proposal may be a much more attractive option in this case because a student loan debt survives personal bankruptcy – unless the student ceased attending school more than seven years before the date of discharge from bankruptcy. This means that if you declare personal bankruptcy, you may end up paying 100 per cent of your outstanding student loans, whereas if you make a successful consumer proposal you may end up repaying approximately 30 per cent of your student loan.

6. Professionals who handle trust funds

7. People who want to be employed in the military or the police, or where a high-level security clearance is required

A consumer proposal and your credit report
The fact that you resolved your debts under a consumer proposal will appear on your credit report and it will be comparable to that of resolving your debts through a repayment plan arranged through credit counselling or making a voluntary debt settlement arranged with your creditor.

PERSONAL BANKRUPTCY

Personal bankruptcy is an option for those who have exhausted all of their other alternatives. It truly is a last resort. In personal bankruptcy you surrender your non-exempt assets – and in the case of high-income earners, a portion of your future income – and most, if not all, of your unsecured debts are forgiven.

In a bankruptcy there are two key dates: the date you file for personal bankruptcy, known as the *date of insolvency,* and the date you obtain your discharge from bankruptcy, your *date of discharge.* After your date of discharge you are referred to as a *discharged bankrupt.* During the period between the date you file for personal bankruptcy and your date of discharge, you are referred to as an *undischarged bankrupt.*

What happens after you file for bankruptcy

Your bankruptcy trustee will prepare the necessary paperwork to file your personal bankruptcy, in consultation with you. Once you file, the bankruptcy trustee informs all the creditors listed in your Statement of Affairs. Any lawsuits your creditors have against you and any wage garnishments will cease. Your judgment creditors will no longer be able to file a writ of execution against you.

IMPORTANT FACT

You will still have to make your child support and spousal support payments even though you've filed for bankruptcy.

With some exceptions, you will have to surrender your property to the bankruptcy trustee, and it will be sold. The proceeds will be distributed to your creditors. You will be entitled to keep property exempt from seizure under provincial and federal law (for more information on exemptions, see my website, www.helpwithcollectioncalls.ca).

In addition, depending on your income and the number of your dependants, you might be required to make surplus income payments to your bankruptcy trustee, which will be distributed to your creditors. The federal government determines the income threshold at which you have to start making surplus income payments, and it increases the threshold every year based on the Consumer Price Index. In October 2009 the threshold for someone with no dependants was a $27,000 annual salary, which meant if you were earning more than that, you'd have to make surplus income payments. The longer it takes you to obtain your discharge, the longer you will be making surplus income payments. And the greater your income, the more you will have to pay.

PRACTICAL TIP
If you will have to make surplus income payments when you file for personal bankruptcy, you might want to make a consumer proposal instead.

In September 2009 the federal government made some changes to laws regarding bankruptcy. The ramifications of these changes remain to be seen. What is clear is that anyone who is required to make surplus income payments will now find it much more costly to file for personal bankruptcy, because they will have to make surplus income payments for 21 months instead of 9 months. Filing for personal bankruptcy becomes less attractive under these changes. To obtain more information about the relevant income threshold for surplus income payments and how much money you might have to pay, you can speak to a bankruptcy trustee.

Obtaining a bankruptcy discharge
After you file for personal bankruptcy, it will be anywhere from 9 to 36 months before you obtain your bankruptcy discharge. The length of time it takes you to obtain a discharge from bankruptcy will depend on a combination of three factors: (1) whether you have previously filed for personal bankruptcy, (2) whether you will be required to make surplus income payments, and (3) whether your personal bankruptcy is opposed.

Although your creditors aren't able to oppose your bankruptcy filing, they are able to oppose your discharge from bankruptcy, and if they do it could take even longer to get it. Having said that, relatively few bankruptcies are opposed. The most common reasons that creditors might oppose a bankruptcy are these:

1. They believe you had the ability to file a consumer proposal instead of bankruptcy.
2. They believe you did not fully disclose your assets.
3. They want to extend the bankruptcy period and request that you pay more money to your bankrupt estate, with the money to be distributed to your creditors.

If one or more of your creditors oppose your bankruptcy, a discharge hearing will be held in bankruptcy court. You will be required to attend, and the opposing creditor and your trustee will also attend. The bankruptcy judge will allow you and the creditors to make a statement and answer questions, and then she will determine whether any conditions will be imposed on your discharge, such as requiring you to pay more money, or to remain an undischarged bankrupt for a longer period of time.

PRACTICAL TIP

If you are worried that a creditor might oppose your discharge from bankruptcy, or if you do not want to attend a bankruptcy discharge hearing in bankruptcy court, it may be prudent to file a consumer proposal instead.

In September 2009, the federal government changed the law concerning eligibility for obtaining a discharge from personal bankruptcy. Now, some people, particularly modest- to high-income earners, and those applying for bankruptcy a second time, will remain undischarged bankrupts much longer.

What happens after you receive your bankruptcy discharge
Most, but not all, of your unsecured debts are forgiven when you obtain your discharge from bankruptcy. The following debts are *not* forgiven:

1. Spousal and child support obligations
2. Student loans where you ceased attending school full-time less than seven years ago
3. Court fines
4. Debts involving fraud

A bankruptcy discharge does not relieve you of your legal obligations to pay your secured creditors. If you own an automobile, for example, and you continue to make your monthly payments on your automobile lease or purchase, you should be able to keep your car.

PRACTICAL TIP

Once you obtain your Certificate of Discharge from your bankruptcy trustee, send a copy of both your Statement of Affairs and your Certificate of Discharge to both Equifax and TransUnion. This will ensure your credit report is updated.

Once you are discharged from personal bankruptcy, you can apply for credit. A note concerning your bankruptcy will appear on your credit report for approximately the next seven years in the case of a first bankruptcy, and for fourteen years in the event of a second bankruptcy.

Advantages of filing for personal bankruptcy
1. You might be able to eliminate most of your unsecured debt. This is the most important advantage of filing for personal bankruptcy.

2. You are able to get credit after you obtain a discharge from bankruptcy (but don't forget that it will be difficult to get credit while you're waiting for your discharge). Some people will tell a bankruptcy trustee that they want to file for personal bankruptcy because a used car dealer has informed them that they cannot currently obtain a car loan due to poor credit but as soon as they obtain a bankruptcy discharge the dealer will grant them a loan. The dealer knows that the car loan will be secured, and all the discharged bankrupt's unsecured debts will be discharged, so, strange as it may seem, some car lenders would actually prefer that you file for bankruptcy before providing you with a car loan. The lender knows that once the bankrupt receives his discharge all of his prior unsecured debts will be discharged and that the lender will have collateral for his car loan.

People for whom personal bankruptcy isn't a good option
Personal bankruptcy might not be an attractive option to a variety of individuals:

1. People earning more than $30,000 or $40,000 a year, who will have to pay surplus income payments until their bankruptcy discharge.

2. People with significant equity in their homes. If you file for personal bankruptcy, your residence may be sold if you have equity in your home, and the sale proceeds distributed to your creditors. However, when you file for personal bankruptcy, you will not necessarily lose your home. Some provinces exempt a certain dollar amount of equity in a principal residence and/or land from seizure.

3. People with significant assets. When you file for personal bankruptcy, you must surrender all your non-exempt property to the bankruptcy trustee; then this property is sold and the proceeds are

distributed to your creditors. The only property you get to keep is property exempt from seizure under provincial law (see my website, www.helpwithcollectioncalls.ca).

4. People with large student loans who ceased to attend school full-time less than seven years ago. When you file for personal bankruptcy, your student loans are not discharged. They survive your bankruptcy unless you ceased to attend school more than seven years prior to your date of filing for bankruptcy.

5. People who handle trust money as part of their jobs or professions. These people might not be able to keep their jobs if they were to file for personal bankruptcy. This would include bankruptcy trustees and lawyers and might include a variety of firms that maintain trust accounts, including collection agencies, debt settlement firms, and credit counselling agencies.

6. People who have already filed for personal bankruptcy. Individuals who file for bankruptcy a second time may have to make surplus income payments for an extended period of time.

7. People who do not want their financial problems to be a matter of public record indefinitely. If you file for personal bankruptcy, it will be a matter of public record, available to anyone who wishes to do an insolvency search on a government database.

IMPORTANT FACT

The Office of the Superintendent of Bankruptcy maintains a registry of the names of people who have obtained a Certificate of Discharge from bankruptcy. It is possible for a member of the public to do a name search and confirm that a specific individual has successfully filed for personal bankruptcy *at some point in the past.* It currently costs about $8 to conduct an insolvency search.

People for whom personal bankruptcy may be an ideal solution
Personal bankruptcy may be an ideal solution for a person who is overwhelmed by debt and falls into one or more of the following categories:

- Has a low income
- Has minimal or no assets
- Has significant tax liabilities
- Has had no prior bankruptcies
- Has insufficient income to make a consumer proposal

Your credit report and personal bankruptcy
If you have filed for personal bankruptcy for the first time, it will appear on your credit report for seven years following your bankruptcy discharge. If you file a second time, it will appear on your credit report for 14 years.

CHAPTER 20

CHOOSING THE APPROPRIATE OPTION FOR RESOLVING YOUR DEBTS

We've now covered the eight options for dealing with your unsecured debts. You might be able to use more than one at the same time, using one for some debts and a second for others. You might also choose to try one option for a while and, depending on the results, change course and try something else. An example will help illustrate this.

Robert, age 50, divorced, lives in Vancouver. He has his own chartered accounting practice. He earns $150,000 a year and lives in a condominium, which he owns. Robert has lost a significant amount of money in the stock market and some investments he made in commercial real estate. His condominium is worth $400,000, but because he refinanced his property at the top of the market he owes a total of $500,000 on the first and second mortgages on the property. Robert owes the Canada Revenue Agency $22,000 and he owes $200,000 to two chartered Canadian banks, Bank A and Bank B, for two $100,000 personal loans. He pays support to his ex-wife, who used to work in his office as his receptionist. Robert has no significant assets other than his home. His business has been valued at $20,000.

Robert wants to avoid bankruptcy at all costs because declaring bankruptcy will have an impact on his chartered accountant licence. Robert has $2,000 a month available to deal with his debt situation. He decides to pay his $22,000 debt with the Canada Revenue Agency over 12 months in instalment payments of $2,000 each. Robert decides to use the Silverthorn Lite debt settlement strategy to deal with his $200,000 in unsecured consumer debt. In the first 12 months Robert will not have any money available to deposit into his debt settlement war chest, because it's being used to pay the Canada Revenue Agency. If he can set aside $2,000 a month after that, he will have the following amounts in the future:

Month 24	$24,000
Month 36	$48,000
Month 48	$72,000
Month 60	$96,000
Month 61	$100,000

By month 51 Robert will have saved $100,000, 50 per cent of his $200,000 in unsecured consumer debt.

In month 6 Robert is sued by Bank A for $100,000. In month 13 Robert has a stroke and is off work for six months, during which time he does not earn any income and he is no longer able to pay any of his bills. In month 19 Bank A obtains a judgment against Robert for $100,000. Robert decides to do a consumer proposal. He is eligible to do so because he is insolvent, meaning that the total dollar value of his debts exceeds his assets. In addition, due to his stroke, he is currently unable to meet his financial obligations as they become due, so he meets the two-part insolvency test required for a consumer proposal. Robert's administrator files a consumer proposal offering to pay his creditors 30 cents on the dollar over four years. This proposal is rejected and Robert files an amended consumer proposal for 35 cents on the dollar over five years, which is accepted. This means that under his consumer proposal Robert will have to pay his creditors 35 per cent of $200,000, or

$70,000. Furthermore, he will be making 60 monthly instalments to his administrator of $1,166.67, an amount that totals $70,000.

In month 1 Robert took advantage of two different options for dealing with his debts. He used instalment payments to pay his $22,000 debt owing to the Canada Revenue Agency, and he also employed the Silverthorn Lite debt settlement strategy to deal with his $200,000 in unsecured consumer debt. In month 19, due to two major developments – a $100,000 judgment against him and the fact that he was unable to earn any income for six months – Robert was able to take advantage of a consumer proposal. When Robert returns to work, provided he remains healthy, he should be able to set aside approximately $2,000 a month for his debts. This is more than enough to enable him to make his $1,166.67 monthly payments to the trustee.

I've come up with nine questions you might find it helpful to ask yourself before you decide which option or options to use to resolve your current debt situation.

1. HAS THE STATUTE OF LIMITATIONS EXPIRED ON ANY OF MY UNSECURED CONSUMER DEBTS?

If so, you can choose not to pay these debts. In the unlikely event that you are sued on this debt, you can file a defence raising the expiry of the limitation period as an affirmative defence.

2. WHEN WILL THE STATUTE OF LIMITATIONS EXPIRE ON MY OUTSTANDING ACCOUNTS?

If you live in Ontario, Alberta, or Saskatchewan, and you stop making payments on your unsecured consumer debts, or you have already stopped making payments, you can avoid paying your debt, *provided you are not sued within two years of the date of your default or your last payment.*

If you live in Quebec, and you stop making payments on your unsecured consumer debts, or you have already stopped making payments, you can avoid paying your debt, *provided you are not sued within three years of the date of your default or your last payment.*

If you live in any territory or province other than Ontario, Alberta, Saskatchewan, or Quebec and you stop making payments on your unsecured consumer debts, or you have already stopped making payments, you can avoid paying your debt, *provided you are not sued within six years from the date of your default or your last payment.*

Before the limitation period on your unsecured consumer debt expires, there are two things that you can do to restart the clock on the limitation period on your debt: make a partial payment or provide your creditor with a written acknowledgement of the debt.

3. DOES THIS OPTION HAVE ANY PARTICULAR DISADVANTAGES?

At the end of each chapter outlining your debt resolution options, I outlined its advantages and disadvantages. Let's recap the disadvantages first:

Instalment payments

Paying your debts by instalment might not be an attractive option for you if you are in serious financial straits, in which case you need to avoid paying a debt altogether or eliminate it at significantly less than 100 cents on the dollar.

Silverthorn Lite and Max

The Silverthorn Lite and Silverthorn Max debt settlement strategies may be unattractive to you if you cannot deal with collection calls or you are uncomfortable with the risk of being sued.

Debt management plan

A debt management plan arranged through a *for-profit* credit counselling agency might be unattractive to you because you might be paying more than 120 cents on the dollar to eliminate your debt.

A debt management plan arranged through a *non-profit* credit counselling agency might be unattractive because you might be paying between 100 cents and 115 cents on the dollar to eliminate your debt.

Consumer proposal

A consumer proposal might be particularly unattractive to you because:

1. You will not have access to credit while you are making monthly payments to your creditors.
2. If you are three months in arrears making monthly payments to your creditors, your consumer proposal will be annulled, and while not automatic, personal bankruptcy might be inevitable.
3. You have to include *all* your debts, even those on which the relevant limitation period has expired.

Personal bankruptcy

Filing for personal bankruptcy might be especially unattractive to you for a number of reasons:

1. You still have large student loans to pay off and you ceased being a full-time student less than seven years ago.
2. You own assets worth a significant amount of money.
3. You earn a significant amount of money.
4. You have declared bankruptcy once before.
5. It could affect your current job or profession or will have a negative impact on your future ability to earn a living.

Debt consolidation loan

A debt consolidation loan might not be an attractive option because it is possible for you to borrow money only at an exorbitant interest rate.

4. DOES THIS OPTION HAVE ANY PARTICULAR ADVANTAGES?

Now let's recap some of the advantages of each option.

Silverthorn Lite and Max

If you are able to use the Silverthorn Lite debt settlement strategy successfully, you should be able to eliminate your unsecured consumer debts for somewhere between 20 and 35 cents on the dollar and sometimes less. And unlike a consumer proposal, it might still be possible for you to access credit.

If you are able to use the Silverthorn Max debt settlement strategy successfully, you will have the option of (1) avoiding paying your unsecured debts altogether or (2) eliminating your unsecured consumer debts for somewhere between 20 and 35 cents on the dollar, and sometimes even less.

Debt management plan

A debt management plan arranged through a non-profit credit counselling agency might be particularly attractive if

1. you want to file for personal bankruptcy, you owe a significant amount of money on student loans, and you have yet to cease attending school full-time for seven years,
2. you owe less than $30,000 to your creditors, or
3. you anticipate that your financial position will improve in the future and you do not want to be sued or receive collection calls for the next 24 to 36 months.

I would never recommend arranging a debt management plan with a for-profit credit counselling agency.

Personal bankruptcy

Personal bankruptcy might be particularly attractive because you will be able to eliminate a significant amount of debt, especially in circumstances where you do not have significant assets and you have a low income.

Consumer proposal

A consumer proposal might be particularly attractive if you have significant assets, earn significant income, or personal bankruptcy is unattractive to you for any reason.

Debt consolidation loan

If you are able to obtain a debt consolidation loan in order to pay off your current debts, this might be an attractive way to deal with your debts because it will likely have the least negative impact on your credit rating.

5. IS THIS OPTION AVAILABLE TO ME AT THE PRESENT TIME?

You cannot use debt settlement or a debt management plan to settle most debts owing to the government. Neither a consumer proposal nor personal bankruptcy are available to you unless you are insolvent. A debt consolidation loan might not be an option for you because you are unable to borrow money at the present time.

6. HOW MUCH WILL THIS OPTION COST ME TO RESOLVE MY CURRENT DEBT SITUATION?

Depending on which option you choose, you might be able to resolve your outstanding debts for less than what they originally cost you or you might end up paying more overall, because of interest, for example. Let's take a look at the associated costs.

Options where you pay more than 120 cents on the dollar to eliminate your debt

The most expensive ways to eliminate debt include these:

1. A debt management plan arranged through a for-profit credit counselling agency
2. Borrowing money at a high interest rate to make payment in full, including borrowing from a high-interest credit card or getting a loan from a finance company
3. Instalment payments in which the repayment period is lengthy and the debts have a high interest rate

Options where you pay between 100 cents and 120 cents on the dollar to eliminate your debt
The following options are a little bit cheaper, but still costly:

1. Making payment in full, provided you do not borrow the money at a high interest rate
2. Making instalment payments where the creditor is charging interest at an annual rate of less than 20 per cent
3. Making instalment payments where your creditor freezes interest after your account is six months in default
4. Entering a debt management plan arranged through a non-profit credit agency

Options where you can eliminate your debt for between 85 cents and 50 cents on the dollar
If your consumer debt is somewhere between 6 and 24 months in default, you should be able to settle your overdue account for a lump sum of between 50 cents and 85 cents on the dollar. If your debt has been sold by your original creditor, you might be able to negotiate lump sum settlements for even lower amounts.

Length of Time Debt in Default	Typical Lump Sum Settlement
6 months to 18 months	85 cents on the dollar
19 months to 24 months	65 cents on the dollar
25 months	50 cents on the dollar

Options where you can eliminate your debt for between 50 cents and 35 cents on the dollar

Most large creditors will provide their collection agents with pre-approved settlement instructions to settle accounts at 50 cents on the dollar when they are around 24 months in default (some even sooner, around 20 months, and some later, around 36 months).

Options where you can eliminate your debt for less than 35 cents on the dollar

There are a number of situations in which you can eliminate your debt for 35 cents on the dollar or less:

1. If your debt owing to your original creditor has been in default for 36 months
2. If your debt has been sold by your original creditor, particularly if your debt is more than 18 months in default
3. If you do a consumer proposal

If your debt is more than 18 months in default and you can satisfy your creditor that you will likely never be in a position to pay your outstanding account in full, you might be able to obtain a settlement for less than 35 cents on the dollar.

IMPORTANT FACT
Creditors will occasionally settle debts for incredibly low amounts before they've even been six or seven months in default.

I'm aware of at least one creditor in Canada who was prepared to settle debts at 20 cents on the dollar in 2009 when the accounts were only six months in default. I was also consistently able to settle my clients' debts that were six months in default with one creditor for between 12 cents and 18 cents on the dollar. I've even heard of situations where purchased debt has been settled for as little as five cents on the dollar!

The cost of filing for personal bankruptcy

Our analysis would not be complete if we did not discuss the cost of filing for personal bankruptcy. There are a number of factors to consider:

1. The fee you must pay to your bankruptcy trustee, typically $1,600 to $1,700
2. The dollar value of any non-exempt property that you must surrender to your bankruptcy trustee
3. *If* you are required to make surplus income payments, their total value
4. The dollar value of your student loans if you have not ceased to be a full-time student for a minimum of seven years, because you will still be required to pay them
5. The dollar value of any unsecured debts other than student loans, such as outstanding fines, that are not discharged in a bankruptcy

The cost of using a limitation period to avoid paying a debt

And the cheapest way to deal with a debt is to avoid paying it altogether by waiting for a limitation period to expire.

7. WHAT IS THE IMPACT OF THIS OPTION ON MY ABILITY TO OBTAIN CREDIT?

Don't forget that if you make a consumer proposal, you will not have access to credit while you are making monthly payments to your creditors, which will be for the next several years. If you file for personal bankruptcy, you might be able to borrow money to buy a car after you obtain your bankruptcy discharge.

8. ARE ANY OF THE OTHER OPTIONS ATTRACTIVE TO ME?

Sometimes you might narrow your choices down to two or three options. Review the advantages and disadvantages of each option and then carefully compare them.

9. ARE THERE ANY OTHER OPTIONS I MIGHT WANT TO TRY *BEFORE* THIS ONE?

Anyone who is contemplating getting a high-interest debt consolidation loan, doing credit counselling, making a consumer proposal, or filing for personal bankruptcy should consider using the Silverthorn Max debt settlement strategy *first*. You might be able to obtain favourable results that way, and if it doesn't work for you, you can still do credit counselling, make a consumer proposal, or file for personal bankruptcy.

Granted, one of the disadvantages of both the Silverthorn Lite and the Silverthorn Max debt settlement strategy is that you might be sued. But as we saw in Chapter 8, you might never be sued on your outstanding accounts. In addition, Chapter 9 showed why a creditor who obtains a judgment against you might never be able to recover any money from you anyway. Furthermore, throughout this book I have shown you a number of ways, both practical and legal, you can reduce the odds of being sued or how you might be able to defeat creditors who have obtained a judgment against you. So your potential liability in the event you decide to rely upon the expiry of a limitation period may not be as bad as you think.

CHAPTER 21

TIPS FOR MAKING A PAYMENT ON YOUR DEBT

Some of your debt settlement options involve making payments to your creditor, a collection agency, or a lawyer. Before you make a single payment, there are certain considerations you should be aware of, to protect yourself by ensuring you have adequate proof of payment.

DOCUMENTS RELATED TO MAKING A PAYMENT

When you make a payment to a collection agency, it is important that you can prove a number of facts: that you made your payment, that the collection agency received your payment, and where appropriate, that an outstanding account has been paid or settled in full. You will need to understand the difference between a proof of payment, a receipt, a settlement letter, and a release letter.

If you've mailed a cheque or money order to a collection agency, your *proof of payment* would be a photocopy of your payment, or your cancelled cheque, or your bank statement. Upon request, a collection agency will provide you with a written document acknowledging receipt of a specific amount of money on a particular outstanding account, your *receipt*. A *settlement letter* is a letter written on the collection agency's letterhead, signed by a collection agency employee, stating that the agency is the authorized representative for a named creditor, and confirming that it will accept payment of a specific sum of money by a certain date as settlement of an account in full. A *release letter* is a letter written on the collection agency's letterhead confirming that a specific debt owed by a particular individual to a named creditor has either been settled or paid in full.

IMPORTANT FACT

After you make a payment to a collection agency, it is important that you can prove that you did so. You should keep your proof of payment, receipts, settlement letters, and any release letters that you receive from a creditor, collection agency, or lawyer for safekeeping.

There is always a chance that you will need these documents later. A collection agency might contact you attempting to collect money on an account that you have already paid or settled in full. Ideally, you should have written proof that you have already paid it, so you can simply fax your proof to the collection agency and end the matter.

FORMS OF PAYMENT

A collection agency will often accept a variety of payment methods, including the following:

- Cash
- Money order
- Western Union
- Cheque or series of postdated cheques
- Credit card

- Bank transfer
- Internet and telephone banking
- Authorized withdrawal from bank account

There are different implications for paying by each of these methods, which we'll review below.

Cash

You will need to exercise caution if you want to make a cash payment to a collection agency. Collection agencies typically have a payments window on their premises where you can make a payment in person. If you do this, make sure you obtain a receipt and that it includes your name, the collection agency's name, the creditor's name and account number, the date, and the amount of your payment.

Large collection agencies usually have a trust account at one or two major chartered banks. If so, you can make a cash payment on your overdue account at a bank branch near your home or workplace. A collector can provide you with the account number where your payment should be deposited. When you go to the bank, speak to the teller and confirm the name of this account to ensure that your payment is being deposited into the collection agency's trust account and not some other account, such as that of the collector's best friend. You should also obtain a receipt from the teller that includes your name, the creditor's name and account number, the date, and the amount of your payment.

There have been cases of fraud in Canada where a consumer wants to make a cash payment and a collector advises the consumer that Joe from ABC courier company will pick up the cash payment that afternoon. In fact, Joe is the collector's friend and the two split the payment. Therefore, you should never make a cash payment unless you do so in person at the agency's payments window or by making a deposit into the collection agency's trust account through a bank teller at a financial institution.

Money order

If you have the cash to make your payment, you could also go to your financial institution or a Canada Post franchise and purchase a money order. It is important that you write your name and your account number on your money order so that your payment is credited to your account. You can then send it to the collection agency by regular mail, Xpresspost, or courier.

PRACTICAL TIP

If you are sending a payment to a collection agency using certified funds (money order, bank draft, or certified cheque), I recommend you do so using Xpresspost or a courier. If you send a money order and it is lost in the regular mail, it can be very difficult to get your money back. It is also faster this way and you'll be able to track the envelope containing your payment.

Western Union

If you have the cash, you can also go to a Western Union location in person and wire your payment to the collection agency. Western Union has locations all across Canada (see www.westernunion.ca). You will be charged a fee for sending money using Western Union, so before you visit a Western Union location you might want to visit its website or call and find out what the service charge will be to make your payment.

Cheque or postdated cheques

Certain issues might arise if you use one or more cheques to make a payment to a collection agency. If you send a postdated cheque, the collection agency may, in error, attempt to cash your cheque earlier than the date on it, and a bank teller may mistakenly process it. There is also a possibility that if you provide a collection agency with a postdated cheque for June 3 there will not be enough money in your chequing account on June 3. If you are going to provide a collection agency with a series of postdated cheques, consider obtaining some overdraft protection on your chequing account to reduce the odds of bouncing a cheque. A cheque is a promise to pay.

IMPORTANT FACT

If you provide a cheque to a collection agency and it is not honoured, the agency can try to cash it up until six months from the date on your cheque, at which point it is stale-dated.

Collection agencies routinely forward dishonoured cheques to the consumer's bank branch requesting that the cheque be certified. Banks refer to this practice as *sending a cheque out for collection.* Once your dishonoured cheque is received at your branch, a clock begins to run, typically ten days in duration. During this period if sufficient funds are in your chequing account to cover the dishonoured cheque, your branch will certify your cheque and the collection agency will receive this certified cheque. A cheque will become stale-dated six months after the date on the cheque, after which it cannot be certified. It is unlikely that collection agencies will attempt to certify cheques for less than $150 to $200 because they incur service charges for doing so.

Sending a cheque to a collection agency has a number of consequences. First, if you are sued your cheque could be introduced into evidence as an admission of your indebtedness. Second, your cheque could be treated as a written acknowledgement of your debt, which would restart the clock on the limitation period on your debt.

Credit card

Most collection agencies in Canada are not able to accept credit card payments. However, what collection agencies cannot do directly, they attempt to do indirectly. A collection agency could encourage you to make a payment by credit card to a related company or the agency's lawyer. You should confirm the name of the company or lawyer that will be accepting your payment on behalf of your creditor.

In some situations, typically for smaller amounts of money, credit card payments can be made with your verbal authorization. In other cases, usually involving larger amounts of money, a collection agency should obtain your written authorization before accepting a credit card payment.

PRACTICAL TIP

If you want to make a credit card payment to a collection agency using your credit card, you should insist on written authorization, to reduce the potential for fraud. The collection agency would typically fax you a form containing the necessary details regarding your account and requesting written authorization.

Granting a bill collector authority to withdraw money from your bank account

I would discourage you from giving a collection agency authority to withdraw money from your bank account. I recall speaking to one consumer who gave a collection agency permission to make a one-time withdrawal from his bank account for $100. Subsequently, without the consumer's permission, the collection agency withdrew more than $500 on two occasions, which resulted in the consumer's account going into overdraft and incurring interest charges and penalties.

HOW TO DEAL WITH UNPROFESSIONAL BILL COLLECTORS

Not every bill collector you interact with is going to act above-board, as I hope you never have to find out. They might engage in *illegal* behaviour that violates a provincial licensing statute. Sometimes their behaviour might be so outrageous that it contravenes the Criminal Code, in which case it would be described as *criminal* behaviour. Part Five is dedicated to helping you deal with this sort of unprofessional bill collector, whether it's someone employed by a collection agency, by your creditor or a debt purchaser, or even by a law firm.

First, you'll need to identify what sorts of behaviour are unprofessional, illegal, or criminal. We'll address this in Chapter 22, "Identifying Bill Collector Misconduct." If you are, or think you are, the victim of unprofessional conduct by a bill collector, you have a number of options:

- First, you might want to collect evidence against the collector (Chapter 23).
- Have a collector charged with a criminal offence under the Criminal Code (Chapter 24).

- Make a complaint against the bill collector to one or more government regulators, to senior management at the collection agency, or to your creditor (Chapter 25).
- Commence a lawsuit against a bill collector, your creditor, or a combination thereof (Chapter 26).

CHAPTER 22

IDENTIFYING
BILL COLLECTOR MISCONDUCT

As you will see in the following case, sometimes bill collectors engage in misconduct during the course of their work, so in this chapter I will explain what they're allowed to do and what they aren't. This is useful because if bill collectors break the law in their dealings with you, you might be able to take advantage of this fact. Depending on the action you take, collectors might stop calling you, they might face consequences, and in some instances, you might even be entitled to financial compensation.

This is an actual case that illustrates the lengths to which some collectors will go to collect a debt.

Mark Tran graduated from the University of Toronto in 1996. Like many Canadians, he had a student loan. Following graduation, he obtained a contract position and began making payments on his Ontario student loan. After the contract ended, he was unemployed for eight months, and during that time his obligations to repay his student loan were suspended. In 1997 Mr. Tran obtained a full-time position as a financial analyst with James P. Marshall Inc., an investment consulting company. Mr. Tran soon contacted the financial institution through which he had obtained his student loan, and he was advised to deal directly with the government. Mr. Tran wrote letters to the Ontario government in an attempt to resume paying his student loan, but he received no response.

In 1999, a Mr. Spina contacted Mr. Tran about his student loan, identifying himself as a government employee with the Ontario Management Board. In fact Mr. Spina was a collector at a collection agency called Financial Debt Recovery Ltd. Collectors employed by Financial Debt Recovery Ltd. began calling Mr. Tran at his workplace. The collectors not only spoke to Mr. Tran, they also spoke with his co-workers and company executives, including the company president. These telephone calls did not stop until Mr. Tran sued Financial Debt Recovery Ltd. in 2000.

In her decision, the trial judge found that the collection agency's employees made a significant number of harassing telephone calls to Mr. Tran's workplace from June of 1999 to March of 2000. These tele-phone calls included profanity, threats of physical harm to Mr. Tran, verbal abuse, and malicious lies. For example, an individual named Mr. Papatetrou had called the president of James P. Marshall Inc., introduced himself as a lawyer with the government of Ontario, and advised the company president that Mr. Tran was interviewing for a job with another employer. Mr. Papatetrou also stated that the Sheriff would come to the company's offices within 24 hours to serve a court order concerning money owed by Mr. Tran. In fact, Mr. Papatetrou was not a lawyer employed by the Ontario government, but a collec-tor employed by Financial Debt Recovery Ltd. All of Mr. Papatetrou's statements about Mr. Tran were untrue.

The final straw came one day in late March of 2000 when Financial Debt Recovery Ltd. made seven phone calls to reception at James P. Marshall in a half-hour period. The receptionist said she would call the police if the firm received any more phone calls, and the calls finally stopped. The incident was reported to senior management and Mr. Tran was advised to take some action to deal with these phone calls.

The calls to Mr. Tran's workplace were not only stressful for him but also affected his compensation. The year before the collection calls began Mr. Tran received a large raise and a significant bonus. After the collection calls started, Mr. Tran received no raise and no bonus.

Mr. Tran did not hire a lawyer. Instead he arranged to sue Financial Debt Recovery Ltd. on his own, for damages of $15,000. The trial judge found that she would have awarded $40,000 in damages were it not for a $25,000 limitation on damage awards under certain court rules.

WHY WOULD A COLLECTOR ACT IN AN UNPROFESSIONAL MANNER?

Three factors contribute to why a significant percentage of bill collectors in Canada today act in an unethical, unprofessional, and illegal manner. The first is greed, which is an integral part of everyday life at a collection agency. The second is a collection agency's overriding fear of losing a major client. And the third is a lack of effective government regulation.

You would think that if a provincial regulator wanted to modify a collection agency's behaviour it would suspend or revoke the collection agency's licence or prosecute and fine it. But in the 12 years that I worked in the collection industry, I never heard of a collection agency of any significant size having its licence suspended or revoked for unprofessional behaviour. In fact, I can think of only one thing that could genuinely change a collection agency's behaviour: the loss of a major client, such as a chartered Canadian bank.

The 30 biggest collection agencies in Canada collect the lion's share of large creditors' accounts. Large creditors do not use the services of a single collection agency. They typically use anywhere between 5 and 15 collection agencies on first assigns, a completely different group on second assigns, and yet another group on third assigns.

A large creditor will evaluate its various agencies over a specific time period called a *competitive race*. In some instances, collection

agencies have daily access to reports on how much money is collected by each agency in a particular competitive race. Collection
agencies that perform well will receive more business in the future.
In contrast, a collection agency that performs poorly runs the risk
of losing a client's business altogether, which could be devastating
financially. This environment encourages collection agencies, both
strong performers and poor performers, to take liberties with the
law in their efforts to do as well as possible in a competitive race.

Collection agencies that are doing poorly in a competitive race
are under tremendous pressure to collect more money. This fact is
communicated to every individual on the collection floor, from the
senior executive in charge of collections, to collection managers,
supervisors, and front-line collectors. The situation is particularly
serious for a collection agency facing the prospect of placing dead
last in a competitive race involving its largest client. A large collection agency that loses a major client might lay off anywhere
between 25 and 100 employees over the space of a few days. It
should come as no surprise, then, that a collection agency that is
in danger of losing a large creditor as a client will not be concerned
about whether its collectors were too aggressive or broke the law
collecting money from members of the public.

Collection agencies earn commissions, a percentage of the
money collected on behalf of their clients. Collection agencies set
commission revenue goals for the agency each month as well as a
monthly quota for each collector. Collectors are typically paid a
base salary, and they usually get a bonus if they collect more money
than their monthly quota. For any collector except the most recent
hires, a collector's bonus might be a significant percentage of his
monthly paycheque. Any collector who does not meet his monthly
quota runs the risk of losing his job or being assigned to a desk the
following month, where it is virtually impossible to earn a bonus.
It is also common for collectors who do not meet their monthly
quota to be dismissed.

IMPORTANT FACT

The compensation system used throughout the collection industry encourages collectors employed by collection agencies to act in an overly aggressive manner and to break the law.

I am not aware of any collection agency that financially penalizes a collector who generates a complaint or whose conduct gives rise to a lawsuit against the agency. Collectors who harass consumers, are abusive, and routinely break the law put more pressure on consumers and therefore should be able to collect more money from them than those who comply with the law. In 2007 an Ontario consumer in *Paulin v. P.C.M. Collections Ltd.* successfully sued a collector and a collection agency for $440,000. The collector had faxed material to the consumer's workplace containing fabricated correspondence indicating that the consumer was a criminal and a person of poor moral character, which led to the consumer being fired. At trial, the president of the defendant collection agency described the defendant collector as the agency's best collector.

That is an extreme example, but if you are in a similar situation, you will need to know what to do. First, you need to be able to identify when a collection agency is breaking the law, so this chapter will introduce you to some of the most important laws collection agencies must comply with.

IMPORTANT FACT

This chapter gives an overview of prohibited collection practices. For much more detailed information about prohibited collection practices in your province, see my website, www.helpwithcollectioncalls.ca.

It is possible that a bill collector's conduct is so outrageous that you could have criminal charges laid against her, and Chapter 24 is devoted to this. The lion's share of this chapter will deal with conduct that is prohibited under provincial law regulating collection agency conduct. But first we will briefly discuss two other types of violations that could affect you: violation of privacy laws and violation of human rights legislation.

THIRD PARTY DISCLOSURE AND VIOLATIONS OF PRIVACY LAWS

You are entitled to privacy under a number of laws. This means your creditors cannot disclose that you owe a debt to anyone except those persons who are legally obligated to pay a debt: you, and in some cases a co-signer. However, there are a few exceptions to this general rule. First, if you inform your creditor that you are represented by an agent, your creditor can disclose the existence of your debt to your agent. Second, if your creditor sues you, to some extent, your privacy will be compromised. If your creditor's lawsuit goes to trial, anyone sitting in the courtroom will hear the details of your debt. Finally, if your creditor sues you *and* obtains a judgment against you, your creditor would then have the right to inform your employer or your bank about the existence of the judgment at the time it attempted to obtain a wage garnishment.

If a bill collector discloses the existence of your debt when he has no lawful right to do so, the bill collector is said to have committed a *third party disclosure,* which is illegal. A third party disclosure could arise in a variety of circumstances. For example, let's say you live with three roommates and you broke your promise to make a payment on an outstanding debt. A collector might leave you the following type of voicemail message:

Collector: This is Bob Green from ABC Collection Agency. You promised to have a $500 payment into my office yesterday by noon. Today is the 25th of the month. I need your payment into this office before the 30th of the month.

In this example, if any of your roommates listened to this voicemail message there would be a third party disclosure because someone other than the person legally responsible for paying a debt (you) was informed of the existence of the debt. If a collector really wants to try to harm your relationship with your employer, he can telephone your human resources department and imply that a wage garnishment is imminent. The conversation might sound something like this:

Collector:	Hello, are you the person responsible for doing payroll?
HR Dept. Employee:	Yes.
Collector:	Does John Smith work at your firm?
HR Dept. Employee:	Yes.
Collector:	Are you the person responsible for processing wage garnishments for employees at your company?
HR Dept. Employee:	Yes.
Collector:	Okay, that's good to know. I'll make a note of that.

It is illegal for a collection agency to disclose the existence of a debt to anyone other than the person legally responsible to pay an account. This type of dirty trick is not only illegal, it is reprehensible. An employee might get fired or have his relationship with his employer irreparably harmed because of these types of calls. If you are fired because of any communications a collection agency has made to your employer, you might have a significant claim for monetary damages against the collector responsible for the communication, the collector's employer, as well as the creditor on whose behalf the collector was attempting to collect the debt. In Chapter 26 I address the issue of commencing a lawsuit seeking monetary compensation.

I can recall a situation where a collector arranged to have a demand letter sent to the consumer's workplace and the correspondence was marked private and confidential. The creditor in question was a provincial government. When the consumer complained to the creditor, the provincial government demanded a meeting with the collection agency, at which the government representative advised the collectors that under no circumstances could a written demand for payment be sent to a consumer's workplace due to possible third party disclosure.

If you have been the victim of a third party disclosure by a bill collector, you might be in a position to make a written complaint to two different government regulators: the government agency responsible for administering privacy laws in your province and, if you have been the victim of third party disclosure by a collection agency, the licensing administrator responsible for regulating collection agencies in your province (see Appendix C, "Collection Agency Licensing Administrators").

VIOLATIONS OF HUMAN RIGHTS LEGISLATION

Some bill collectors might make inappropriate or offensive comments about an individual's race, religion, ancestry, family situation, sexual orientation, or mental or physical disability in the course of a telephone call. These comments might be illegal under provincial human rights legislation, and you might be in a position to make a complaint to a human rights commission, known in some provinces as a human rights tribunal.

During my years representing collection agencies, on more than one occasion I represented a collection agency that was the subject of a human rights complaint, something I would describe as a major annoyance to a collection agency because responding to such a complaint involves a considerable amount of time, energy, and expense. Furthermore, where there is a human rights complaint against a collection agency, a collector, or the agency's client, *the consumer essentially gets a free shot.* I've never heard of a consumer who brings a frivolous or unsubstantiated human rights complaint being penalized in any manner for doing so.

I once defended a collection agency in circumstances where the consumer claimed a collector called him, a Quebec resident, a "frog." I spent 15 to 20 hours preparing a response to this complaint, reviewing the agency's notes, interviewing any collectors who had spoken to the consumer, and reviewing the agency's phone logs, and I am sure my client's staff spent at least four hours providing me with background information. Subsequently, the Ontario Human Rights Commission determined that the consumer's complaint did not warrant a formal hearing. The consumer who made the complaint just happened to be employed as a collector at another collection agency, and his credit report revealed that virtually all his personal accounts were more than six months in default. He was a real piece of work and knew how to work the system in order to avoid paying his bills. As soon as the collection agency learned of the existence of the human rights complaint, all collection calls to him were suspended indefinitely.

If you have had your rights under provincial human rights legislation infringed, you should, without delay, contact the human rights commission in your province as well as the province from which the collection call was made. If you wait several months to make a complaint, this will undermine your credibility and, in some cases, the human rights commission may refuse to even consider a complaint if too much time has elapsed between the date of the incident and the date of your complaint. Appendix D, "Canadian Human Rights Commissions and Tribunals," lists contact information for human rights commissions in Canada.

When you first call a human rights commission, you might speak to a front-line counsellor who will determine if your complaint is one falling within the commission's jurisdiction. If it does, you need to complete the appropriate forms, setting out the details of your complaint. A copy of your complaint will be provided to those who are the subject of your complaint, typically a collection agency, possibly one or more collectors, and, in some cases, your creditor. Once senior management learns that a consumer has made a human rights complaint against its collection agency, the agency will probably cease all further collection calls on the account.

VIOLATION OF PROVINCIAL LAW REGULATING COLLECTION AGENCIES

Each province and territory in Canada has one specific law dealing with both the licensing and regulation of the conduct of collection agencies. Each of these laws contains what I will refer to as a *code of prohibited collection practices,* a list of conduct by collection agencies and their employees that is illegal in that province or territory. These laws vary across Canada. For example, it is illegal for a collector to phone a Newfoundland resident at her place of employment. In contrast, if you are an Ontario resident, it is legal for a collector at a collection agency to call you at your workplace.

IMPORTANT FACT
Each province and territory in Canada has its own code of prohibited collection practices for collection agencies and collectors. The law regulating the conduct of collection agencies and its employees is not uniform across Canada.

This lack of consistency in the law regulating the conduct of collectors across Canada creates major challenges for collection agencies and contributes to a significant number of violations of provincial law. A collector working with other collectors on a dialer may speak to individuals living in 70 households in nine different provinces during an eight-hour shift. If I were to work a day as a collector on a dialer, I could easily violate provincial law at least once or twice during an eight-hour shift – and I have written a book on the topic. How could you expect a new hire at a collection agency who has undergone a one-week or two-week training program to be familiar with the code of prohibited collection practices in an environment where they are taking incoming calls without interruption from the residents of up to ten provinces and three territories in no particular order?

Collection agency and collector licensing requirements

Each province and territory requires that a collection agency contacting its residents have a collection agency licence. For example, if you are a Manitoba resident, any collection agency contacting you must be licensed as a collection agency in Manitoba. It is illegal, therefore, for a collection agency to communicate with you unless it has a collection agency licence in the province or territory in which you live.

In addition, every province except for Quebec, Newfoundland, and Prince Edward Island requires individual collectors to be licensed. If you live anywhere in Canada except for Quebec, Newfoundland, Prince Edward Island, and the three territories, any collector employed by a collection agency is breaking the law unless he is licensed as a collector in your province. You should be able to confirm whether a specific individual is licensed as a collector by phoning the office of the provincial licensing administrator.

Providing written notice before starting collection calls

Five provinces – British Columbia, Ontario, Quebec, Newfoundland, and Nova Scotia – as well as the Northwest Territories require that a collection agency mail you a written notice before it starts making collection calls to you. The written notice should advise you that the collection agency is acting on behalf of a specific creditor concerning the collection of a specific debt. The remaining five provinces, the Yukon, and Nunavut do not have this written notice requirement.

Duty not to collect accounts that are not owing

The law in most provinces imposes a duty on a collection agency not to attempt to collect a debt unless a person is legally responsible to pay the debt. I can think of three specific situations where a bill collector could violate this duty. First, collection agencies have a duty to suspend all collection activity on a file once they have reason to believe the collection agency is making a demand for payment from the wrong person. Second, it would be illegal for a collector to attempt to collect a debt from a family member if the family member is not legally responsible to pay the debt. A family member might be jointly responsible to pay for a debt where they are a co-signer on a loan or they have a supplementary credit card. Finally, since a debt is *extinguished* in British Columbia after it has been in default for six years, it would be illegal for a bill collector to demand payment of an account from a B.C. resident if the consumer had not made a payment on a consumer debt for more than six years and had not acknowledged the debt in writing during the past six years.

How onerous this duty is varies by province. In Nova Scotia, for example, it is illegal for a collection agency to attempt to collect a debt unless the agency first satisfies itself that a debt is, in fact, owing. Given the manner in which collection agencies operate in Canada today, this law must be broken virtually every weekday. In Quebec a collection agency is legally required to cease all collection activity on a file after it is advised that a consumer is not the debtor. If you live in a number of other provinces, including Ontario, once you advise a collection agency that you are not the debtor the collection agency must suspend all collection activity until it can confirm that you are the debtor. This involves the collection agency requesting additional information or documents from its client.

Law against making false or misleading statements
Virtually every province and territory in Canada has a law making it illegal for a collection agency to make false or misleading statements to you. In fact, collectors in Canada routinely make false or misleading statements to consumers, and two senior executives

at collection agencies who have more than 20 years' experience in senior positions at some of the largest collection agencies in Canada recently confirmed this fact with me.

IMPORTANT FACT

Collectors employed by collection agencies may break the law in as many as one-quarter to one-half of all collection calls to consumers. The single greatest form of misconduct by collectors is making false or misleading statements to consumers.

The most common false or misleading statement by a collector involves the threat to sue you. As much as one-half to three-quarters of all the consumer debt in Canada today is owed to Canada's major chartered banks. Today, virtually none of Canada's big banks grant collection agencies authority to sue the thousands of files sent to a collection agency. This means that when a collector threatens to sue you on the phone, there is a good chance the collector is breaking the law.

Collectors often make false or misleading statements about the consequences of your failure to pay an account. It is quite common for a collector to inform a consumer that he will have the Sheriff come to your residence sometime in the next few days to seize some of your personal property, obtain a wage garnishment, seize money in your bank accounts, or place a lien on your home, if your account remains unpaid. These types of statements by a collector are almost always illegal.

Collectors usually make any false or misleading statements verbally. In some instances, a collection agency may be so out of control that it might make false or misleading statements in writing in one of its collection letters. One of my clients received such a collection letter dated May 12, 2009, from a collection agency in Ontario by the name of Unik Collectrite Inc. that essentially said my client would be subject to a garnishment if her account was not paid within three days.

Your creditor is not able to obtain a wage garnishment, seize your personal property or money in your bank account, or place a lien on your property unless it has first sued you *and* obtained a judgment against you. In the event that you are sued, it would be necessary for your creditor to serve legal documents on you commencing a lawsuit and you would have the opportunity to file a defence and have a trial. There is no guarantee that your creditor would be successful at trial. Even if your creditor did obtain a judgment against you, there is no guarantee that it could recover any money from you. Your creditor might not be able to identify your place of employment, any of your assets that legally could be seized to satisfy a judgment, the branch where you have bank accounts, or real property in which your name is on the title.

In other words, this statement clearly violates provincial law.

Violations of provincial law involving collection letters
Some provinces require that collection agencies submit all their collection notices to the provincial regulator for approval before they can be used. They don't always do this. Most provinces also prohibit collection agencies from using an imitation court form when attempting to collect a debt. And in 2008, the Ontario Registrar of Collection Agencies advised agencies operating in Ontario that it was unacceptable for them to retain lawyers to send collection letters *of any kind whatsoever* in which the lawyer failed to disclose the name of the collection agency hiring her.

Prohibited times for making collection calls
Each province bans collection calls from collection agencies on certain days of the year and during certain times of the day. In most provinces, collection agencies are prohibited from making calls on statutory holidays and on Sundays. Furthermore, in most provinces they are not permitted between 9 p.m. and 7 a.m. or 8 a.m., local time. For a more detailed summary, see Appendix B, "Times When Collection Calls Are Prohibited."

IMPORTANT FACT

Just because a collection agency is calling you during *permitted times* doesn't necessarily mean it's legal for the collection agency to call you.

The following list summarizes the circumstances when it is illegal for a collection agency to make collection calls during *permitted times:*

1. You have exercised your right to stop collection calls. If you have exercised a right to stop collection calls, the fact that a collection agency is calling you during permitted times is irrelevant. It is still illegal for a collection agency to call you.

2. A collection agency is calling you at work and workplace calls are not permitted in your province. Several provinces ban or severely restrict a collection agency's right to call consumers at their workplace.

3. A collection agency is calling you on your cellphone and cellphone calls are not permitted in your province. In Canada cellphone customers typically pay for their incoming calls. The law everywhere but Alberta, Quebec, and Nunavut prohibits a collection agency from communicating with a consumer if it results in the consumer incurring an expense. Therefore, it is illegal for a collection agency to call a resident of Canada, excluding those provinces named, on their cellphone, unless they do not pay for incoming calls.

In fact, collection agencies routinely violate this provincial law, and the scale of the violation is only increasing with the exponential growth in cellphone use across Canada. In 2008 just under three-quarters of all Canadian households reported having at least one cellphone and 8 per cent of all Canadian households were cellphone-only users.

4. You live in British Columbia, Saskatchewan, or Manitoba and the collection agency is infringing on your right to privacy under the provincial Privacy Act. If you or your lawyer were to write a letter threatening to sue a bill collector on this basis, it might stop calling you or at least call you less.

5. A collector is calling more frequently than is legally permitted. Two provinces, Alberta and Ontario, have a specific standard for how often a collection agency can legally call their residents. In these two provinces, a collection agency is permitted to phone you only three times in a consecutive seven-day period. However, virtually every province has a law prohibiting a collection agency from harassing you. If a collection agency is calling you more than once a day, I believe most regulators responsible for regulating collection agencies in Canada would have cause for concern and your situation would warrant some attention from them.

IMPORTANT FACT

If you are receiving more than one unwanted collection call a day from a collection agency, you may want to consider making a written complaint to the body responsible for licensing and regulating the conduct of collection agencies in your province (see Appendix C).

CHAPTER 23

GOING ON THE OFFENSIVE

If you are going to take action against a collection agency or a collector, you can do a number of things to improve your chances of success. First you will need to figure out exactly who is calling you, and then you can gather evidence to increase the credibility of your complaint. This chapter will tell you how.

IDENTIFYING THE COLLECTION AGENCY AND THE COLLECTOR

It may seem obvious, but it is difficult to take action against an unprofessional collection agency unless you can identify the name of the collection agency. Collectors who phone you do not always leave their names or the names of their employers.

If you live in British Columbia, Ontario, Quebec, Nova Scotia, or Newfoundland, provincial law requires collection agencies to provide you with a written notice before commencing collection calls. These notices must contain the agency's name, its address, its telephone number, the name of your creditor, an account number, and the balance owing.

Otherwise, you might be able to identify the collection agency calling you by contacting the creditor on whose behalf the calls are being made. Creditors are permitted to send your outstanding account to only one collection agency at any given point in time. If your creditor is large, you might need to contact the creditor's national or regional collection centre to identify the name of the agency that has your account. If you are receiving collection letters from a law firm and a collection agency over the same timeframe, the odds are that the collection agency has hired the lawyer to send you the collection letter and the lawyer does not have any meaningful involvement with your account.

If you receive a recorded message from a collection agency, the message will likely include a telephone number requesting a return call concerning an important matter, and it might quote some file number. It will not mention the collection agency's name, due to privacy issues. However, you might be able to identify the collection agency by calling the number provided. For a list of the names, addresses, and contact phone numbers for some of the largest collection agencies in Canada, visit my website, www.helpwithcollectioncalls.ca.

In most provinces, once a collector has confirmed that she is speaking with the debtor, she is required to disclose certain information: the collector's name, the name of her employer, the creditor's name, the account number, and the balance owing. If you are speaking with a collector on the phone and you have identified yourself as the person the collector is looking for, you can insist that the collector disclose this information to you. I recommend that you request this information in the following order: (1) the name of your creditor, (2) the account number in question, (3) the balance owing, (4) the name of the agency, (5) the collector's name and telephone number. If the collector refuses to disclose this information, end the call and make a note of the date and time, and what took place.

If you receive a phone call from someone you suspect is a collector, you should be able to identify the name of the collector's employer without disclosing any information about yourself. Simply advise the caller that you are busy right now but if he leaves his name and phone number you will call him back later. You might want to try calling the person after business hours to see if you can learn the name of his employer. The collection agency's name might be disclosed in the person's voicemail greeting or in a general voice mailbox. If you know the collector's name, you might be able to identify his employer by contacting the provincial licensing administrator's office in your province. In most provinces, individual collectors are licensed and the licensing administrator has a list of their names on file. In some provinces, such as Ontario, you can confirm on a provincial government website that a particular individual is licensed as a collector.

If you are going to take action against a collection agency, it is helpful, but not absolutely necessary, to know the name of the agency's employees who have spoken to you. The most efficient way to obtain this information is to ask the individuals for their name and telephone number during your telephone conversation. Write it down.

A small percentage of collectors do not use their real names when they are working; instead they use a *desk name* or an alias. Every province in Canada licenses individual collectors with the exception of Quebec, Newfoundland, and Prince Edward Island. In those provinces where collectors must be licensed, they must normally use their real name when dealing with the public. Sometimes a collector will use a desk name because her name is awkward to pronounce, recognize, or spell. If a collector is legally permitted to use a desk name or an alias in a province that licenses individual collectors, this desk name should be registered with the provincial licensing administrator.

MAKING YOUR ALLEGATIONS OF MISCONDUCT MORE CREDIBLE

If you are going to take action against a collection agency in response to unprofessional or illegal conduct, it will be helpful for you to have some evidence to support your allegations. The more information and supporting material you have, the more credible your allegations will be. There are three key ways you can gather this information: (1) maintain a journal, (2) record telephone calls with collection agency employees, and (3) make a request under Canadian privacy laws to discover what information a collection agency has on you.

Maintaining a journal

If you are receiving collection calls, it is a good idea to maintain a journal recording the dates and times of telephone calls concerning your account. You should also make a note of the names of the collector, collection agency, the creditor, and the account number, and summarize what was said. You should also make an entry in your journal for phone calls that you make in connection with this matter.

The more detailed the notes the better. In at least one reported court case, *Anderson v. Excel Collection Services Ltd.*, a trial judge commented that he wished a consumer had made notes of his conversation with collectors: "It would have markedly advanced his [the plaintiff's] case if he had taken down notes of telephone conversations. Mr. Anderson did not keep a log. Excel appeared to have done so."

It is important for you to have a record of communications between you and the collection agency, because the collection agency will have its own record. They use specialized software containing a separate file for each one of their accounts, which serves as a chronological record of all activities on an account. When a collector speaks with you on the phone, he will enter information onto the note lines on your account summarizing what was said during the conversation. In addition, a collector will enter note lines on your file – or is supposed to anyway – when he speaks to someone other than you about your account. Collection agencies rely on the information in these note lines to respond to complaints, lawsuits, and prosecutions. You should have your own record too.

Recording your telephone calls

Some collection agencies might record some or all of their telephone conversations with consumers. Before your telephone call can be recorded by a collection agency, you should be advised that your call may be recorded. You have the option of requesting that it not be or refusing to speak to the collector if it is. Telephone calls are more likely to be recorded if you are dealing with one of the bigger collection agencies operating in Canada, because they can afford the expense associated with recording and storing hundreds of thousands of telephone calls.

You might find it odd that a collection agency would record calls, since it's expensive and the recording might contain proof that a collector acted improperly. However, some large creditors insist that collection calls be recorded as a way to improve the chances that collectors working on their behalf conduct themselves at high standards of professionalism. If a consumer makes a complaint to a creditor, the creditor may request a copy of the recording. If a collector's behaviour during a recorded telephone conversation is outrageous, some collection agencies will make the excuse that no recording is available due to some technical problem. I have also been told by reliable sources that some collection agencies even doctor a recorded telephone conversation to make the original version sound less outrageous.

The majority of complaints consumers make against bill collectors are about telephone conversations. Often it's your word against the collector's. A collector might be able to avoid disciplinary action or avoid a lawsuit simply because you lack proof to support your allegations. That's why it's important for you to record your calls rather than rely on a collector to do so – especially since the agency could erase or doctor the tapes. Your allegations of a bill collector's misconduct will be much more credible if you can produce a recording of your telephone conversation.

PRACTICAL TIP

It is legal for you to record a telephone conversation with a bill collector even though you do not disclose the fact that you are doing so. If you are going to record your calls, I recommend you do not notify the collector – unless your goal is to encourage the collector to act in a more civilized manner toward you.

Collectors employed by creditors are often the worst offenders when it comes to abusive behaviour. You might find it helpful to record their abusive phone calls, because there may be several radio stations that would be pleased to play your recording on the air. Or if you play it for a manager at the creditor in question, the agency might decide to stop calling you.

If you are interested in recording telephone conversations with bill collectors, you can go to a retail source such as The Source by Circuit City to purchase the appropriate equipment. I like the Panasonic IC Recorder (model RR-US550). It enables you to record conversations directly from your telephone as an MP3 file, which you can easily download onto a computer. To record your calls, you will also need one or two other pieces of equipment – the exact ones depend on whether you have a corded phone or a cordless phone.

If you familiarize yourself with the law in your province regulating collection agencies and you are recording your calls, you might be able to lure an inexperienced or unsuspecting collector into making an illegal statement. You might, for example, ask a collector if the collection agency is going to sue you. Chances are the collection agency has not obtained permission to sue you, so if she says yes, the collector has broken the law. You can use this to file a complaint, as we will see in Chapter 25.

USING PRIVACY LAWS TO FIND SKELETONS IN A BILL COLLECTOR'S CLOSET

Canadian privacy laws might help you show that a collection agency has engaged in some form of misconduct. These laws permit consumers to request copies of their personal records *from a collection agency* – and it is required to provide them. These records may include recorded telephone conversations pertaining to your account or your file on the collection agency's software, including note lines. These records might contain the "smoking gun" that provides irrefutable proof supporting your allegations of misconduct.

The value of making a privacy request

The records you obtain under privacy laws can be used for a variety of purposes. A recording of a telephone conversation between you and a collector may be devastating for a collection agency, because it could support laying criminal charges, be the basis for a successful civil lawsuit, or support a credible complaint to a government regulator, your creditor, or senior management at the collection agency. This might be the case, for example, if a collector threatened to kill an individual or cause them bodily injury.

A copy of a collection agency's note lines from your account might also support your claim of agency misconduct. The note lines provide a detailed summary of the agency's activity on your file and are supposed to show the dates and times of every phone call made in connection with your account, and a record of all the relevant outgoing and incoming correspondence related to it. The note lines do not contain a verbatim transcript of what was said during a telephone call. Collectors enter date and time-stamped notes during a telephone conversation or immediately thereafter, summarizing the gist of the conversation and often using abbreviations. A collector who speaks with you or a member of the public without entering a note line could face serious disciplinary sanctions.

Some examples where note lines showed misconduct include the following:

- Brian, a resident of Victoria, B.C., made a successful complaint to the B.C. Business Practices and Consumer Protection Authority, relying on the agency's note lines to show that numerous collection calls were made to him despite the fact that the agency never sent him a letter advising him that it was the authorized collection agent for his creditor with respect to collection of a particular debt.
- An agency's note lines showed that a collector made 50 phone calls to Wanda, a Halifax resident, when Wanda's lawyer had previously sent a registered letter to the collection agency advising it that he was representing her. Under the Nova Scotia Collection Agencies Act the collection agency was permitted to contact only Wanda's lawyer in the future and not Wanda. A criminal charge of making harassing telephone calls under subsection 327(3) of the Criminal Code was warranted.
- Bill, a resident of Hamilton, Ontario, made a successful complaint to a chartered bank that resulted in a collection agency losing market share, after the note lines revealed that a collection agency made repeated phone calls to Bill's employer and relatives despite the fact that the collection agency had a current telephone number for him at both his home and his workplace. This was a violation of the Ontario Collection Agencies Act.
- John, a Newfoundland resident, was able to sue a collection agency successfully when the date and time-stamped notes on his account showed that a collector phoned him on several occasions at his workplace during business hours. The Newfoundland Collections Act prohibits any calls from a collection agency to an individual's workplace.

Where to make your request for personal information

In a perfect world we would have one privacy law across Canada that applied to private sector organizations such as collection agencies. Unfortunately, as many as four different privacy laws may be involved when you are seeking records containing your personal information from a collection agency.

A few years ago, the federal government enacted the Personal Information Protection and Electronic Documents Act (PIPEDA). The purpose of this law was to provide Canadians with certain privacy rights and to enable individuals to access any personal information that an organization possessed on them. This law allowed provinces to opt out of PIPEDA by passing their own privacy laws; Alberta, British Columbia, and Quebec all enacted their own privacy laws, so PIPEDA does not apply to collection agencies operating in those provinces. However, things get complicated when a collection agency located in one province makes phone calls to a resident of another province. Depending on the province in which you live and where a collection agency's office is located, it may be necessary for you to make a request for records under two different Canadian privacy laws.

If you are going to make a request for records, you should first determine the privacy law that applies in the province where you live and the privacy law that applies where the collection calls and collection notices are originating from. In some cases, only one will apply. In other cases, two different ones might apply. If you are unsure, request records under both privacy laws.

The privacy laws in Alberta, British Columbia, and Quebec are based on the same principles as those contained in PIPEDA. In Alberta, the privacy law is the Alberta Personal Information Protection Act, in British Columbia it is the British Columbia Personal Information Act, and in Quebec it is known as An Act Respecting the Protection of Personal Information in the Private Sector. For contact information for the federal privacy commissioner and the privacy commissioners in British Columbia, Alberta, and Quebec, see Appendix E, "Privacy Commissioners in Canada."

The remainder of this chapter deals with making a written request to a collection agency for records containing your personal information under PIPEDA. Information on requesting records under the B.C., Alberta, and Quebec privacy laws may be obtained from the respective government websites.

Making a written request under PIPEDA

When you contact a collection agency requesting records containing your personal information under PIPEDA, your request should be in writing. First, contact the collection agency's head office and request the name of the person responsible for PIPEDA compliance, their title, and mailing address. Under the Act, a collection agency is required to designate one or more individuals as responsible for handling requests for personal information. Furthermore, the collection agency has a legal obligation to provide the name of the employee responsible for PIPEDA compliance, if you request it. In addition, if you advise a collection agency that you require help preparing a request for personal information, it has a legal duty to assist you.

PRACTICAL TIP

Your PIPEDA request should be sent to the collection agency by courier, Xpresspost or registered mail so you can prove the collection agency received it.

Sample PIPEDA Request Letter

(Your name)
(Your mailing address)
(City, province, postal code)

(Date)

SENT BY REGISTERED MAIL:

(Name of collection agency)
(Mailing address)
(City, province, postal code)

Attn: (name of person at agency responsible for PIPEDA compliance)

Dear Sir/Mme.;

Re: (Your name)
(Name of your creditor)
(Your account number)

I am writing you in connection with the above-noted account.

At some point your collection agency was attempting to collect this account from me. This will confirm that, under the Personal Information Protection and Electronic Documents Act (PIPEDA), I wish to obtain a copy of all records containing my personal information.

More specifically, I am requesting copies of the following records:

- Any recorded telephone conversations with respect to the above-noted account involving employees of your collection agency;
- The contents of your electronic file on my account, including but not limited to the note lines;
- The contents of any hard copy file in connection with the account;
- Outgoing correspondence with respect to my file, including any documents sent by regular mail, courier, facsimile (including fax cover sheets), or e-mail;
- Incoming correspondence with respect to my file, including any documents received by regular mail, courier, facsimile, or e-mail;
- Any credit reports in your possession.

I understand that under PIPEDA, your collection agency has 30 days from the date you receive this letter to provide me with any records containing my personal information, except where you satisfy the conditions for a 30-day extension, in which case you have 60 days from the date of receiving this letter to provide me with copies of the requested personal information.

Sincerely,
(Your signature)
(Your name)

Records that might be requested under PIPEDA

You should be entitled to a copy of the following material under a written PIPEDA request for personal information, provided it exists:

- The contents of your electronic file on the collection software used by the collection agency, including the note lines and information on your file provided by the creditor or its agent
- Contents of any hard copy file in connection with your account
- Any recorded telephone conversations pertaining to your account
- Incoming or outgoing correspondence concerning your account (mail, e-mail, and facsimile, including fax cover sheets)
- Any credit reports in the collection agency's possession

How long a collection agency has to respond to a PIPEDA request

Under PIPEDA, a collection agency has 30 days from the date it receives your written request to provide you with copies of its records in response to your request. A collection agency has a limited right to extend this deadline for an additional 30 days, if it is unable to meet it. However, before the original 30-day deadline expires, it must notify you that it will require an additional 30 days to comply with your request, provide reasons it needs additional time, and advise you of your right to make a complaint to the federal privacy commissioner over its decision to rely on an extension.

If a collection agency fails to provide the material you requested within the 30- or 60-day period, it is deemed to have refused your request, in which case you can file a written complaint to the federal privacy commissioner under PIPEDA. Your complaint should be sent to the following address:

The Office of the Privacy Commissioner of Canada
112 Kent Street
Ottawa, ON K1A 1H3

You can also telephone the Office of the Privacy Commissioner of Canada toll-free at 1-800-282-1376. For more information about PIPEDA, visit the Privacy Commissioner of Canada's website at www.privcom.gc.ca.

CHAPTER 24

LAYING CRIMINAL CHARGES AGAINST A BILL COLLECTOR

This chapter provides information about Criminal Code offences that a collector could conceivably commit. You may be the victim of *illegal* conduct by a collector or a collection agency, where they have violated provincial or federal law. If this involves the commission of an offence under the Criminal Code, then a collector's conduct can be characterized as *criminal* and criminal charges may be warranted. If you have been the victim of a criminal offence, you should call your local police department.

HARASSING TELEPHONE CALLS

A collector could be convicted of making harassing telephone calls under subsection 372(3) of the Criminal Code. I will limit my comments to a collector's phone calls to a debtor. However, there is no reason that a collector could not be convicted for making harassing telephone calls to someone else, such as a relative or receptionist at an individual's workplace. To successfully prosecute a collector for this offence, the prosecutor will need to prove the following three elements:

1. The collector is making repeated phone calls;
2. The collector intends to harass another person; and
3. The calls are being made without lawful excuse.

A collector cannot be convicted under this section for making a single phone call, regardless of how unconscionable his behaviour is. The collector must make two or more phone calls.

The prosecutor must also prove the collector's intent to harass. A collector could be convicted of this even if he does not say anything to the person answering the phone. In *R. v. Sabine,* a 1990 case in New Brunswick, the accused made 14 telephone calls to one number in an eight-minute period without speaking to anyone answering the telephone. The accused was convicted, even though he did not have a particular person in mind as his target.

Obviously, not every telephone call a collector makes to a consumer concerning a delinquent account is made with intent to harass. The prosecutor must be able to establish the collector's intent to harass, relying on statements made by the collector, the frequency of the telephone calls, or a combination thereof. Based on the *Sabine* case, it would appear that an intent to harass might be inferred if a collector were to make more than 10 phone calls to one phone number in less than 30 minutes.

The most difficult element for the prosecutor to prove in a harassing telephone calls prosecution against a collector is that the calls are being made "without lawful excuse." Subject to certain limitations, collectors do have a lawful excuse to call a consumer under the provincial licensing statute in the jurisdiction where the consumer resides. However, there are a number of situations in which a collector would be making collection calls *without lawful excuse*:

- Where the collection agency employing a collector is not licensed as a collection agency in the province where you live

- Where a collector is not licensed as a collector in the province where you live (all provinces require that collectors have a valid collector's licence except Quebec, Prince Edward Island, and Newfoundland)
- Where a collector is making telephone calls on days when calls are not permitted in the province where you live
- Where a collector is calling you outside the hours when calls are legally permitted in the province where you live
- Where a collector is calling you and it has failed to comply with an obligation to provide written notice prior to commencing collection calls (only residents of British Columbia, Ontario, Quebec, Nova Scotia, and Newfoundland are entitled to this prior written notice)
- Where a collector is calling you in circumstances where you have exercised a statutory right to prohibit collection calls from that agency, as outlined in Chapter 3 (these statutory rights are available only to residents of British Columbia, Alberta, Ontario, Quebec, and Nova Scotia)
- Where the collector's conduct is so unconscionable that it is beyond the scope of conduct legally permitted under the provincial licensing statute in the province where you live
- Where a collector is calling you more than 10 times in a single day, particularly where the calls are made during a short period of time
- Where the collector is calling you in circumstances in which the collector is violating the law (Canadian privacy law, laws specifically regulating collection agency conduct, or human rights legislation)

To obtain a conviction for making harassing telephone calls under subsection 372(3) of the Criminal Code, the prosecutor does not need to prove that you fear for your safety or that of another person.

CRIMINAL HARASSMENT

Criminal harassment is a more serious offence under the Criminal Code than making harassing telephone calls. In order to convict a collector for criminal harassment under section 264 of the Criminal Code, the prosecutor must prove the following four elements:

1. The collector is making repeated phone calls;
2. The collector must intend to harass someone by making these calls, or be so reckless that it is reasonable to conclude that someone is being harassed by the collector's conduct;
3. The collector must be acting without lawful authority; and
4. The collector must cause another individual to fear for his or her own safety, or the safety of another person, and this fear must be reasonable.

In other words, in order to obtain a conviction for criminal harassment, the prosecutor must prove the three elements required for a conviction under harassing telephone calls, plus one additional element: the accused must cause another individual to fear for his or her safety or the safety of another person, and this fear must be reasonable. This means that, in some circumstances, the prosecutor will be in a position to obtain a conviction on the charge of harassing telephone calls but not on a charge of criminal harassment.

THREATS TO PHYSICALLY HARM SOMEONE

Under section 264.1 of the Criminal Code, Uttering Threats, it would be a criminal offence for a bill collector to threaten you or anyone else with physical harm or death.

CONVEYING A FALSE MESSAGE

A collector could also conceivably be convicted of the crime of conveying a false message under subsection 372(1) of the Criminal Code, which reads as follows:

> Everyone who, with intent to injure or alarm any person, conveys or causes or procures to be conveyed by letter, telegram, telephone, cable, radio, or otherwise information that he or she knows to be false is guilty of an indictable offence and liable for imprisonment for a term not exceeding two years.

In order for the prosecutor to successfully prosecute a collector for conveying a false message under subsection 372(1) of the Criminal Code, he would need to prove the following four elements:

1. A collector must provide false information to someone;
2. The collector must know that this information is false;
3. The false message must be made by means of a telephone call, letter, telegram, cable, radio, or otherwise; and
4. By making the false statements, the collector intended to harm or alarm someone.

It is possible that a collector might be convicted of conveying a false message in circumstances where he threatened an unsophisticated individual with imprisonment or deportation should the person fail to pay the outstanding account. It is not necessary for the prosecutor to prove that anyone was injured or suffered alarm as a result of the collector's statements to obtain a conviction for conveying a false message. However, it would likely be easier to get charges laid and obtain a conviction if it would be reasonable for a person to be alarmed or someone did, in fact, suffer an injury.

IMPERSONATING A POLICE OFFICER

Under section 30 of the Criminal Code, it is an offence to impersonate a police officer when you are not one. In the debt collection context, I can certainly envision how a collection agency employee might be tempted to pretend to be a police officer for the following purposes:

- To obtain the debtor's address or telephone number from the debtor's friends, relatives, family members or employer;
- To encourage a debtor to return a voicemail message;
- To motivate someone without Canadian citizenship to pay a debt by threatening to have the person deported unless a debt is paid.

MAKING ARRANGEMENTS TO HAVE CRIMINAL CHARGES LAID

If you believe that a collection agency employee has committed a Criminal Code offence, you should contact your local police department and provide it with all the relevant details. You can have the police listen to voicemail messages left by a collector or a recording of a telephone conversation between a collector and you or another individual. You might also want to give the police copies of collection letters you have received.

If for some reason your local police force chooses not to lay criminal charges, you may want to meet with a local justice of the peace, to see if he or she will arrange to have criminal charges laid. You should be able to see a justice of the peace by simply showing up at the local courthouse where criminal matters are heard during business hours. There is usually a lineup to see a justice of the peace so I suggest you arrive at the courthouse around 1:30 p.m. You should bring any supporting documentation with you, including tapes of voicemail messages, recordings of telephone conversations, and letters from the collection agency. Your goal is to be able to present credible evidence that a crime has been committed. It would be prudent for you to provide the justice of the peace with the specific section or sub-section of the Criminal Code that you believe has been contravened.

IMPORTANT FACT

It is a serious matter to lay criminal charges. If you do so and your conduct is malicious or unwarranted, you may find yourself in civil court or having criminal charges laid against you.

CHAPTER 25

MAKING AN EFFECTIVE COMPLAINT AGAINST A BILL COLLECTOR

If you have been the victim of *illegal* behaviour rather than *criminal* behaviour, an effective way to handle the situation is to make an official complaint. There are five different bodies to which you might want to make a complaint: (1) the creditor, (2) a collection agency's senior management, (3) a regulating body, (4) a privacy commissioner, and (5) a human rights commission. There is also one unofficial way you could make your complaint heard, and that is to go to the media with your story. This chapter will cover each of these options and how you would go about filing your complaint.

MAKING A COMPLAINT TO YOUR CREDITOR

IMPORTANT FACT

If you have been the victim of unconscionable behaviour by a collection agency, one of the most effective things you can do to "push back," short of suing, is to make a credible written complaint to the creditor on whose behalf it is acting.

Major creditors such as credit card issuers, chartered banks, large retailers, and utilities such as telephone companies and cable and Internet service providers spend millions of dollars promoting their brand. They do not want their image tarnished by the actions of collectors working at an unprofessional collection agency. Your written complaint to your creditor could result in major headaches for the collection agency and any collectors involved, and it could even result in the agency losing future business from that creditor.

Large creditors award new business, involving tens of thousands of accounts, on the basis of an agency's performance over the past few months. The most important factor a creditor considers when evaluating agency performance is its ability to collect money. However, when a creditor is evaluating a collection agency's performance in a competitive race, it will also consider the agency's complaints history. A collection agency with a poor track record may drop in rankings in a competitive race and may even be dropped altogether.

When you make a complaint to a creditor, it is important that you send it to the appropriate person. If the creditor in question is a chartered bank, you should not complain to the teller at your local bank branch; your letter should go to someone in senior management. Most large creditors have either a national collection centre or several regional collection centres, and your complaint letter should go to a senior executive there. You should be able to obtain this information by visiting your creditor's website. It might also be necessary to make a few calls to obtain the name, title, and mailing address of a senior executive responsible for forwarding your creditor's overdue accounts to collection agencies.

Your complaint should be in writing and it should contain as much detail as possible, as well as copies of any supporting material. You should keep copies of all your correspondence with the creditor. You might want to provide your creditor with a copy of any recordings of telephone conversations illustrating a collection agency's misconduct.

Reasons you might not want to complain to your creditor

As a general rule, if a collection agency has violated provincial law regulating collection agencies, I would not recommend that you initially make a complaint to your creditor. If you do, the creditor may simply recall your account from the collection agency and assign it to another one, in which case you will start receiving collection calls all over again. It may be better to simply make a complaint to senior management at the collection agency itself. You can inform the agency that if you get one more collection call you are going to make a written complaint to the creditor. This will likely result in the agency effectively suspending collection activities on your account. If your account is a consumer debt, each day that goes by, the date when the limitation period on your debt expires draws closer.

However, you might want to complain to the creditor immediately if you are receiving collection calls in which the collection agency's conduct is outrageous or it continues to contact you after you have advised it that you are not, in fact, the debtor.

MAKING A COMPLAINT TO A COLLECTION AGENCY'S SENIOR MANAGEMENT

There are a couple of reasons you might wish to make a complaint to a collection agency's senior management about its conduct: you may want the agency to stop contacting you, or you want it to discipline an unprofessional employee working for it. Depending on how serious your complaint is, management may feel it should cease all collection activity on your file to avoid making the situation any worse than it already is. The agency may feel that if it continues communicating with you, things may escalate to the point where you make a complaint to the provincial licensing administrator or to the creditor. In some instances, a collection agency may suspend all collection activity in response to your complaint because it has concerns that any further communications may result in a lawsuit against the agency.

When you write a letter to a collection agency to complain about its conduct, you should address your letter to the president or a senior executive at the company's head office. You can obtain the name of the president or chief executive officer by phoning the main switchboard at the collection agency's head office. Your complaint should provide as much detail as possible and state precisely and clearly the problem. If the agency has violated a particular law, refer to the law, and quote the specific section of the statute, if you know what it is.

In your letter, inform the recipient that, if you receive any further collection calls from the agency, you will make a written complaint to the creditor on whose behalf the agency is contacting you, as well as the provincial licensing administrator in your province.

If your complaint is simply sent to the collection agency, and not addressed to a specific senior executive at head office, you may waste your time sending the letter. It is also probably a waste of your time to call a collection agency and ask to speak to a collector's supervisor or manager to make a complaint. If you do, you might end up speaking to the collector's best friend sitting at the next workstation or someone whose primary motivation is to use your call as an opportunity to persuade you to pay your account.

Send your letter of complaint by registered mail, courier, or by Xpresspost and keep a copy of it, as well as any responses from the agency.

MAKING A COMPLAINT TO A REGULATOR

Another option is to make a written complaint to the body regulating whoever has been acting in an unprofessional manner: the body regulating your creditor, a collection agency, or a collection lawyer.

Complaints to those regulating creditors

British Columbia appears to be the only province in which the conduct of creditors collecting their own debt is regulated by provincial law. The definition of "collector" in the British Columbia

Business Practices and Consumer Protection Act is broad enough to include anyone collecting a debt, including a creditor, a debt buyer, a collection agency, and a law firm or their employees. This means that creditors in British Columbia must abide by the same code of prohibited collection practices that apply to collection agencies.

Complaints to those regulating collection agencies

Collection agencies are regulated in each province and territory by a licensing administrator, and they typically generate more complaints than other types of business regulated by provincial governments. Residents of Alberta, Ontario, and Nova Scotia can submit their complaint online. Residents of British Columbia and Saskatchewan can obtain a copy of a complaint form online, print the form, complete it, and mail in their complaint. In the remaining provinces and territories, residents can submit their complaint in writing to the provincial licensing administrator's office. For a complete list of the licensing administrators to which you would make a complaint, see Appendix C, "Collection Agency Licensing Administrators."

Your complaint should be as detailed as possible, and include copies of any relevant voicemails and recorded telephone conversations. If you did not record the telephone conversation, you can provide the provincial licensing administrator with a summary, from memory, of what was said during the call or provide a photocopy of any notes you made during the conversation or immediately thereafter. If you believe the collection agency may have recorded this telephone conversation, you should advise the provincial licensing administrator. If your complaint involves written correspondence, you should provide copies.

IMPORTANT FACT

When a collection agency receives a complaint, it will often suspend all collection activity on the file. Even so, the problem might not be over, because your creditor could send your account to a new collection agency, starting the calls all over again. If this new collection agency breaks the law, you might be able to take action again that could result in it suspending activity on your account.

The licensing administrator will request a written response to your complaint from the collection agency as well as from any employees you refer to in your complaint. The licensing administrator may take some disciplinary action against a collector or his employer or both. A collector could have his licence suspended for a few days.

IMPORTANT FACT
If you want to make a complaint against a collection agency, the fact that you owe the debt the agency is attempting to collect is irrelevant.

If a collection agency does not abide by the licensing statute regulating its conduct, it faces potential prosecution and the possibility of having its licence suspended or revoked. The fact that a provincial licensing administrator could potentially suspend a collection agency's licence is a very big stick, especially for large collection agencies. When a large creditor considers doing business with a national collection agency, it will often ask to see a copy of the company's collection agency licences in all ten provinces and three territories. If a collection agency were to have its licence suspended in just one province for a few days, and this was to become public knowledge, it could potentially ruin the collection agency.

Damages for Manitoba and Yukon Residents
If you are a resident of Manitoba or the Yukon, you might be able to recover compensation from a collection agency equal to three times any money wrongfully collected. The agency could have collected from the wrong person or it could have collected from

the right person, but more money than it was lawfully entitled to recover, for instance if it added fees to the balance owing over and above what the consumer owes the creditor.

A Manitoba resident is entitled to triple damages for wrongful collection only where the consumer has actually paid money to a collection agency that was not rightfully owing. In contrast, in the Yukon a consumer is entitled to triple damages if the collection agency collects or *attempts to collect* money that is not rightfully owed. If you believe that you might be entitled to triple damages for wrongful collection, you should provide the details to your licensing administrator. If you are, in fact, entitled to compensation, the administrator will likely contact the collection agency and arrange to have you compensated.

Complaints to those regulating lawyers

If you want to make a complaint against a lawyer or a law firm engaged in debt collection, you can make your complaint to the lawyer's provincial law society. If you are a B.C. resident, you could also make a complaint to the British Columbia Business Practices and Consumer Protection Authority.

MAKING A COMPLAINT TO A PRIVACY COMMISSIONER FOR THIRD PARTY DISCLOSURE

As noted earlier, collection agencies are not permitted to disclose the existence of your debt nor any details surrounding your debt to anyone other than you, except in very limited circumstances (e.g., collection agencies *are* permitted to discuss the existence of your debt with anyone who is also liable for the debt, such as a guarantor on a loan. If a collection agency sued you on behalf of a creditor and obtained a judgment against you, the collection agency might contact your employer about a wage garnishment).

If a collection agency has made a third party disclosure concerning your account, you may want to make a written complaint under the federal Personal Information Protection and Electronic

Documents Act (PIPEDA) or the provincial privacy laws in British Columbia, Alberta, or Quebec (for contact information, see Appendix F, "Privacy Commissioners in Canada"). You can also make a complaint to the provincial licensing administrator in your province.

Where you make a complaint under PIPEDA, the office of the federal privacy commissioner will investigate your complaint, and sometimes, but not always, prepare a report within one year. If the commissioner does, in fact, prepare a report, you normally have 45 days to apply to the Federal Court for a hearing in connection with any matter arising out of the report. A Federal Court hearing your matter has the power to award financial compensation to you, including damages for humiliation.

MAKING A COMPLAINT TO A HUMAN RIGHTS COMMISSION

Sometimes a consumer will make a complaint against a collector and a collection agency under human rights legislation – for instance, if a collector has made some derogatory remarks about the consumer's race, religion, ethnicity, family situation, or sexual orientation. If you want to file such a complaint, you should contact your provincial human rights commission, referred to as a human rights tribunal in some provinces. If collection calls are being made to you from outside your province, it may also be prudent to contact the human rights commission in the province where the collector is situated. For contact information, see Appendix D, "Canadian Human Rights Commissions and Tribunals."

IMPORTANT FACT

A human rights commission may decline to hear complaints if too much time has passed since the alleged misconduct. So if you want to make a complaint under human rights legislation, you should do so without delay.

There may be an initial determination of whether the human rights commission has jurisdiction to deal with your specific complaint. You may be advised that it does not deal with the conduct you are complaining of, or the person you speak to may suggest that you contact a human rights commission in a different province. Complaints to human rights commissions are typically made in writing by filling out certain forms. If you bring a successful human rights complaint, you may end up receiving some type of financial compensation.

TELLING YOUR STORY TO THE MEDIA

If you have been the victim of especially outrageous conduct by a bill collector, you might be able to put pressure on it by telling your story to the media. You will likely have better luck with your local newspaper than your local television or radio station. Your local newspaper may have a reporter with a regular news column dedicated to consumer issues, and you may be able to interest them in writing a story about your situation. If you live in a large city with several newspapers, start with the consumer columnist for the local tabloid as opposed to a newspaper serving a more business-oriented readership.

Canadian TV and radio networks, like CBC and CTV, have consumer advocacy programs and may be interested in doing an investigative report about a bill collector's conduct. Most news organizations have an assignment editor who assigns potential stories to reporters. You will probably have only one or two minutes to convince the assignment editor of the merits of assigning a reporter to do a story on your problem. You might be able to grab an assignment editor's attention by e-mailing them a recording of your telephone conversation with a bill collector. Keep in mind that your story has to compete with major news stories and may never obtain any coverage.

CHAPTER 26

SUING A BILL COLLECTOR

The primary goal of suing a bill collector is usually to obtain financial compensation. Suing a bill collector is a serious matter and it does not always have positive results. If you are unsuccessful at trial, the court may require that you pay a portion of the collector's legal fees, and you will likely be sued yourself for any money owing to the creditor. For many people, commencing a lawsuit involves a great deal of stress and anxiety and likely means taking some time off work.

GROUNDS FOR COMMENCING A LAWSUIT
The amount of money that you might be entitled to should you win your lawsuit will depend on the nature of the collector's actions and the type of harm you have suffered as a result. If you wish to commence a lawsuit in the hopes of obtaining more than about $10,000 in financial compensation, I suggest you only do so in one or more of the following scenarios:

1. Your reputation has been damaged.

2. You have suffered quantifiable economic loss of more than a few thousand dollars as a result of a collector's conduct.

3. You, or someone in your household, has suffered mental or psychological distress as a result of the collector's conduct; the individual concerned must have been diagnosed as having a recognized physical condition or a recognized psychological illness caused by the collector's conduct.

4. You have lost your job as a result of a collector's communications at your workplace.

5. A collector's communications to your workplace have poisoned your relationship with your employer and you can establish a loss of income potential as a result.

6. A collector has disclosed your personal information to others, and as a result, you have suffered some type of economic loss or significant humiliation.

7. A collector has threatened you with physical harm, imprisonment, or deportation.

A *nuisance claim* means that a bill collector has made a nuisance of itself but you have not suffered any damage to your reputation nor economic loss of any significance, and no one in your household has suffered a recognized medical condition or a recognized psychological illness. It's unlikely you'll recover more than $10,000, if anything, in a nuisance claim.

DON'T FORGET THE BIG PICTURE
It is one thing to sue a collection agency when you do not owe any money to the creditor on whose behalf it is acting. It is an entirely different matter if you do owe money to the creditor. If you sue a

collection agency, you should expect that you will be sued for any money owing to its client. It does not make sense for you to sue a collection agency in circumstances where you would be lucky to obtain a judgment against a collection agency for, say, $2,500, if the collection agency is attempting to collect a debt you legitimately owe in the amount of $30,000, or when you have no defence. Sometimes it is best to let sleeping dogs lie.

REPRESENTING YOURSELF VERSUS OBTAINING LEGAL REPRESENTATION

If there is a possibility that your claim against a bill collector is worth more than $10,000, it might be prudent for you to hire a competent civil litigation lawyer or paralegal. My review of the court cases in Canada over the past ten years would suggest that individuals who have sued collection agencies, in circumstances where the individual's claim was worth more than $10,000, have not obtained good results representing themselves. The more your lawsuit is worth, the more it makes sense to hire a legal representative.

You can find a civil litigation lawyer or a paralegal by looking in the Yellow Pages or on the Internet, or by asking friends and acquaintances for a recommendation. Several provinces have a Lawyer Referral Program through which you can obtain 20 or 30 minutes of free legal advice over the telephone.

WORKSHEET: PROFILE OF YOUR CURRENT DEBTS

CONSUMER	DEBT	Debt owing to federal or provincial government	Debt neither consumer debt nor gov't debt
UNSECURED	SECURED		
Back rent at residence where you currently live Money owing on certain utilities where you currently live: Hydro Cable Water Internet Landline telephone Credit cards Personal loans Bank overdrafts Cellphone Student loans owing to a Canadian chartered bank Other	Debt owing to buy or lease your car Your outstanding mortgage Property taxes Secured loans Secured lines of credit Any purchases you made in which you provided collateral List any credit included in a Master Credit Agreement with a lender Mortgage: Lines of credit: Personal loans: Credit cards:	Income tax Government fines Money owing to the government arising from overpayment of government benefits Student loans owing to (1) Federal government (2) Provincial government	Child support Spousal support

The debts that appear in a shaded background are those you may be able to settle for less than 100 cents on the dollar.

TIMES WHEN COLLECTION CALLS ARE PROHIBITED

Jurisdiction	Days and Times When Collection Calls Are Prohibited (all times are local time)
Alberta	(1) On a statutory holiday (2) Between 9 p.m. and 8 a.m.[1]
British Columbia	(1) On a statutory holiday (2) On a Sunday, except between 1 p.m. and 5 p.m. (3) Between 9 p.m. and 7 a.m., Monday through Saturday[2]
Manitoba	(1) On a statutory holiday (2) On a Sunday (3) Between 9 p.m. and 7 a.m., Monday through Saturday[3]
New Brunswick	Between 9 p.m. and 9 a.m., seven days a week[4]
Newfoundland	Between 10 p.m. and 8 a.m., seven days a week[5]
Northwest Territories	(1) On a statutory holiday (2) On a Sunday, except between 1 p.m. and 5 p.m. (3) Between 9 p.m. and 7 a.m., Monday through Saturday[6]
Nova Scotia	(1) On a Sunday (2) Between 9 p.m. and 8 a.m., Monday through Saturday[7]
Nunavut	No restrictions
Ontario	(1) On a statutory holiday (2) On a Sunday, except between 1 p.m. and 5 p.m. (3) Between 9 p.m. and 7 a.m., Monday through Saturday[8]
P.E.I.	Between 9 p.m. and 8 a.m., seven days a week[9]
Quebec	(1) On a Sunday (2) Between 8 p.m. and 8 a.m., Monday through Saturday[10]
Saskatchewan	(1) On a Sunday (2) Between 9 p.m. and 8 a.m., Monday through Saturday[11]
Yukon	(1) On a Sunday (2) Between 9 p.m. and 7 a.m., Monday through Saturday[12]

[1] *Collection and Debt Repayment Debt Repayment Regulations*, Alta. Reg. 194/99, ss. 12(1)(g).

[2] British Columbia *Business Practices and Consumer Protection Act*, S.B.C. 2004, c. 2, s. 118.

[3] Manitoba *Consumer Protection Act*, C.C.S.M. c. C200, ss. 98(j).

[4] *General Regulation – Collection Agencies Act*, N.B. Reg. 84-256, ss. 14(g).

[5] *Collections Regulations*, Nfld. Reg. 90/85, ss. 12(1)(c).

[6] *Debt Collection Practice Regulations*, ss. 12(1)(c).

[7] Nova Scotia *Collection Agencies Act*, R.S. c. 77, ss. 20(1)(i).

[8] General Regulation, R.R.O. 1990, Reg. 74, ss. 22(6).

[9] *Collections Agencies Act Regulations*, R.R.P.E.I. EC450/95, ss. 5(f).

[10] *An Act respecting the Collection of certain debts*, R.S.Q., C. R-2.2, ss. 34(4).

[11] Saskatchewan's *The Collection Agents Act*, R.S.S. 1978 c. C-15, ss. 29(1)(h).

[12] Yukon *Consumers Protection Act*, R.S.Y. 2002, c. 40, ss. 72(c).

There are two reasons you might want to contact a licensing administrator. First, you might want to obtain information. You might, for example, want to confirm whether a collection agency or a collector is licensed in your province. (It is illegal for a *collection agency* to attempt to collect money from you unless it holds a valid collection agency licence in the province or territory in which you live. Furthermore, it is illegal in Ontario, the four western provinces, New Brunswick, Nova Scotia, and the Yukon for *individuals* employed by a collection agency to attempt to collect money from you unless they hold a valid collector's licence in your province or territory.) Second, you might want to file a complaint against a collection agency or a collector, or both.

British Columbia, Alberta, Saskatchewan, Ontario, and Nova Scotia have a special procedure for handling complaints against collection agencies. If you are a resident of one of these five provinces and you wish to make a complaint against a collection agency, you should visit the government website referred to in this appendix and make a complaint using the prescribed form.

ALBERTA

To obtain information about collection agencies, phone Service Alberta at either its Edmonton or Calgary office at the following phone numbers. Alberta residents who wish to make a complaint against a collection agency can do so online, by mail, or by fax. To make a complaint, visit www.servicealberta.gov.ab.ca/1006.cfm, and in the complaint category select "collection practices." You can mail or fax a complaint to the following offices:

For residents with a (780) area code

Service Alberta
North Field Services, Licensing
3rd Floor, Commerce Place
10155 102nd Street
Edmonton, AB T5J 4L4
Tel.: (780) 422-1335
Fax: (780) 422-9106
e-mail: nfs@gov.ab.ca
Attn: Manager, Investigations

For residents with a (403) area code

Service Alberta
South Field Services, Licensing
301, 7015 Macleod Trail South
Calgary, AB T2H 2K6
Tel.: (403) 297-5743
Fax: (403) 297-4270
e-mail: sfs@gov.ab.ca
Attn.: Manager, Investigations

BRITISH COLUMBIA

Collection agencies that attempt to collect debts from residents of British Columbia must hold a valid collection agency licence under the British Columbia Business Practices and Consumer Protection Act (BPCPA). Individuals employed by collection agencies attempting to collect money from B.C. residents must hold a valid collector licence issued under the BPCPA. Those provisions in the British Columbia BPCPA that regulate the conduct of collection agencies and their employees apply to anyone collecting a debt from a resident of British Columbia. Therefore, those provisions of the British Columbia BCCPA that regulate the conduct of collection agencies also apply to creditors, debt buyers, and lawyers engaged in the collection of debts, as well as their employees.

To obtain information about both licensing issues and the regulation of those collecting debts from British Columbia residents, contact the following office:

Business Practices and Consumer Protection Authority
Attention: Inquiry Centre
P.O. Box 9244

Victoria, BC V8W 9J2
Tel.: 888-564-9963
Fax: (250) 920-7181
e-mail: info@bpcpa.ca

To file a complaint under the British Columbia Business Practices and Consumer Protection Act visit www.bpcpa.ca.

MANITOBA
To obtain information about collection agencies or to file a complaint in writing by fax, by mail, or by e-mail, contact the following office:

Consumer's Bureau
Government of Manitoba
258 Portage, Rm. 302
Winnipeg, MB R3C 0B6
Tel.: (204) 945-3975
Fax: (204) 945-0728
e-mail: consumersbureau@gov.mb.ca

NEW BRUNSWICK
You can file a complaint by telephone, mail, fax, or e-mail at the following office:

Ann Sparkes
Enforcement Officer
Department of Justice and Consumer Affairs
Government of New Brunswick
440 King Street, King Tower, Rm. 649
Fredericton, NB E3B 5H8
Tel.: (506) 453-2659
Fax: (506) 444-4494
e-mail: ann.sparkes@gnb.ca

NEWFOUNDLAND

You can file a complaint in writing, by mail, by fax, or by e-mail, to the following office:

Terri-Lynn Taylor
Consumer Affairs Officer
Department of Consumer Affairs
Trade Practices Division
Department of Government Services
Government of Newfoundland and Labrador
5 Mews Place
St. John's, NL A1B 4J6
Tel.: (709) 729-2660
Fax: (709) 729-6998
e-mail: ttaylor@gov.nl.ca

NORTHWEST TERRITORIES

To obtain information about collection agencies or to file a complaint, contact the following office:

Michael Gagnon
Senior Policy Advisor
Consumer Services
Department of Municipal and Community Affairs
Government of NWT
Suite 400, 5201 50th Avenue
Yellowknife, NT X1A 3S9
Tel.: (867) 873-7125
Fax: (867) 873-0609
e-mail: Michael_Gagnon@gov.nt.ca

NOVA SCOTIA

To obtain information about collection agencies or for assistance filing a complaint against a collection agency, telephone Service Nova Scotia at (902) 424-5200 or toll-free at 1-800-670-4357.

To file a complaint against a collection agency visit www.gov.ns.ca/ snsmr/consumer/resolve.asp.

NUNAVUT

To obtain information about collection agencies or to file a complaint, contact the following office:

Leah Aupaluktuq
Senior Consumer Affairs Officer
Department of Community & Government Services
Government of Nunavut
267 Qaiqtuq Building
P.O. Box 440
Baker Lake, NU X0C 0A0
Tel.: (867) 793-3303
Fax: (867) 793-3321

ONTARIO

To obtain information about collection agencies, contact the following office:

Ministry of Consumer Services
Consumer Protection Branch
5775 Yonge Street, Suite 1500
Toronto, ON M7A 2E5
Tel.: 1-800-889-9768
Fax: (416) 326-8665
e-mail: consumer@ontario.ca

Visit www.consumerbeware.mgs.gov.on.ca/esearch/start.do to confirm whether a collection agency or a collector holds a valid licence in Ontario.

For information about filing a complaint against a collection agency, visit www.gov.on.ca/mgs/en/ConsProt/STEL02_168949.html. You can file a complaint online at www.cbs.gov.on.ca/compform/english/complaint.asp, or in writing. If you are going to file a complaint in writing, download the Complaint Form from this website and submit your completed Complaint Form, together with any supporting documentation, by fax or by mail, to the Consumer Protection Branch.

PRINCE EDWARD ISLAND

To obtain information about collection agencies or to file a complaint, you can contact the following office:

Linda Peters
Compliance Officer
Consumer Services Division
Office of the Attorney General
Government of PEI
Shaw Building, 95 Rochford Street
Charlottetown, PE C1A 7N8
Tel.: (902) 368-5653
Fax: (902) 368-5283
e-mail: lmpeters@gov.pe.ca

QUEBEC

To obtain more information about collection agencies or to file a complaint, you can contact one of the following phone numbers for the Consumer Protection Branch or Office de la protection du consommateur, or visit www.opc.qc.ca:

Montreal	(514) 253-6556
Quebec	(418) 643-1484
Trois Rivières	(819) 371-6400
Saguenay	(418) 695-8427
Gatineau	(819) 772-3016

Sherbrooke   (819) 820-3694
Saint-Jérôme (450) 569-7585
Calls from outside Quebec: 888-OPC-ALLO; 888-672-2556

SASKATCHEWAN

To obtain information about collection agencies, contact the following office:

Saskatchewan Justice
Consumer Protection Branch
1919 Saskatchewan Drive, Suite 500
Regina, SK S4P 4H2
Tel.: (306) 787-5550 and toll-free in Saskatchewan at 888-374-4636
Fax: (306) 787-9779
e-mail: consumerprotection@gov.sk.ca

You can file a complaint in writing by mail, fax, or e-mail. To file a complaint against a collection agency, the Saskatchewan Consumer Protection Branch recommends that you call toll-free at 1-888-374-4636 or in Regina at (306) 787-5550. If the staff recommends that you file a formal complaint, visit www.justice.gov.sk.ca/cpb. On the home page, under Resources, click on Forms and then Consumer Complaint Form. On the next page click on the button marked "Open Form." You can forward your completed form to the Consumer Protection Branch.

YUKON

To obtain information about collection agencies or to file a complaint, contact the following office:

Consumer Services
Department of Community Services
Yukon Government
Andrew A. Philipsen Law Centre
3rd Floor, 2130 2nd Avenue

Whitehorse, Yukon Y1A 5H6
Tel.: (867) 667-5111
Fax: (867) 667-3609
e-mail: consumer@gov.yk.ca

If you phone the office, you should ask to speak to a Consumer Relations Officer.

CANADIAN HUMAN RIGHTS COMMISSIONS AND TRIBUNALS

If you wish to make a human rights complaint, you should contact the appropriate office in your province. In most provinces this is the human rights commission. In British Columbia, Ontario, and Nunavut it is called the human rights tribunal. When you contact the office responsible for handling human rights complaints in your province, it might advise you that you can make a complaint to its office or that its office does not have jurisdiction over your complaint, in which case it may suggest an alternative course of action for you. This could include contacting a human rights commission in another province.

ALBERTA

The Alberta Human Rights and Citizenship Commission has two offices serving Alberta residents:

Alberta Human Rights and Citizenship Commission
Northern Regional Office
800 Standard Life Centre
10405 Jasper Avenue
Edmonton, AB T5J 4R7
Tel.: (780) 427-7661
Fax: (780) 427-6013

Alberta Human Rights and Citizenship Commission
Southern Regional Office
Suite 310, 525 11 Avenue SW

Calgary, AB T2R 0C0
Tel.: (403) 297-6561

www.albertahumanrights.ab.ca

BRITISH COLUMBIA
B.C. Human Rights Tribunal
1170 605 Robson Street
Vancouver, BC V6B 5J3
Tel.: (604) 775-2000 and toll-free at 1-866-440-8844
Fax: (604) 775-2020
TTY: (604) 775-2021
e-mail: BCHumanRightsTribunal@gov.bc.ca
www.bchrt.bc.ca/

MANITOBA
The Manitoba Human Rights Commission has three offices serving
Manitoba residents, in Winnipeg, Brandon, and The Pas.

Manitoba Human Rights Commission
7th Floor, 175 Hargrave
Winnipeg, MB R3C 3R8
Tel.: (204) 945-3007 and toll-free at 1-888-884-8681
Fax: (204) 945-1292
TTY: (204) 945-3442
hrc@gov.mb.ca

Manitoba Human Rights Commission
Provincial Government Building
340 9th Street
Brandon, MB R7A 6C2
Tel.: (204) 726-6261 and toll-free at 1-800-201-2551
Fax: (204) 726-6035
TTY: (204) 726-6152

Manitoba Human Rights Commission
2nd Floor Otineka Mall
P.O. Box 2550
The Pas, MB R9A 1K5
Tel.: (204) 627-8270 and toll-free at 1-800-676-7084
TTY: (204) 623-7892

www.gov.mb.ca/hrc

NEW BRUNSWICK

The head office for the New Brunswick Human Rights Commission is located in Fredericton. The New Brunswick Human Rights Commission also serves New Brunswick residents at three regional offices in Moncton, Saint John, and Campbellton.

New Brunswick Human Rights Commission
Head Office
751 Brunswick Street
P.O. Box 6000
Fredericton, NB E3B 5H1
Tel.: (506) 453-2653
Fax: (506) 453-2653
TDD: (506) 453-2911
e-mail: hrc.cdp@gnb.ca (for service in English) and
hrd.cdp@gnb.ca (for service in French)

New Brunswick Human Rights Commission
Place 1604
200 Champlain Street, Suite 320
Dieppe, NB E1A 1P1
Tel.: (506) 453-2301 and toll-free at 1-888-471-2233
Fax: (506) 869-6608
New Brunswick Human Rights Commission
8 Castle Street, 2nd Floor

P.O. Box 500
Saint John, NB E2L 4Y9
Tel.: (506) 453-2301 and toll-free at 1-888-471-2233
Fax: (506) 658-3075

New Brunswick Human Rights Commission
6 Arran Street
P.O. Box 5001
Campbellton, NB E3N 1K4
Tel.: (506) 453-2301 and toll-free at 1-888-471-2233
Fax: (506) 789-2430

www.gnb.ca/hrc-cdp/

NEWFOUNDLAND
Human Rights Commission
Newfoundland and Labrador
P.O. Box 8700
St. John's, NL A1B 4J6
Tel.: (709) 729-2709 and toll-free at 1-800-563-5808
Fax: (709) 729-0790
e-mail: humanrights@mail.gov.nl.ca
www.justice.gov.nl.ca/hrc/

NORTHWEST TERRITORIES
Northwest Territories Human Rights Commission
Main Floor, Laing Building
5003 49th Street
Yellowknife, NT X1A 2P4
Tel.: (toll-free) 1-888-669-5575
Fax: (867) 873-0357
e-mail: info@nwthumanrights.ca
www.nwthumanrights.ca

NOVA SCOTIA

The Central Office for the Nova Scotia Human Rights Commission is located in Halifax. The Commission also has regional offices in Digby, Sydney, and New Glasgow.

If you are calling from within Nova Scotia, you can call the Commission toll-free at 1-877-269-7699.

Nova Scotia Human Rights Commission
Central Office
6th Floor, Joseph Howe Building
1690 Hollis Street
P.O. Box 2221
Halifax, NS B3J 3C4
Tel.: (902) 424-4111
Fax: (902) 422-0596

Nova Scotia Human Rights Commission
Provincial Building
84 Warwick Street
Digby, NS B0V 1A0
Tel.: (902) 245-4791
Fax: (902) 245-7103

Nova Scotia Human Rights Commission
Provincial Building
Prince Street
Sydney, NS B1P 5L1
Tel.: (902) 563-2140
Fax: (902) 563-5613

www.gov.ns.ca/humanrights/

NUNAVUT
Nunavut Human Rights Tribunal
P.O. Box 15
Coral Harbour NU X0C 0C0
Tel.: (toll-free) 1-866-413-6478

ONTARIO
Human Rights Tribunal of Ontario
655 Bay Street, 14th Floor
Toronto, ON M7A 2A3
Tel.: 416-326-2027 in Toronto and toll-free at 1-866-598-0322
Fax: (toll-free) 1-866-355-6099

www.ohrc.on.ca

PRINCE EDWARD ISLAND
PEI Human Rights Commission
53 Water Street
Charlottetown, PE C1A 1A3
Tel.: (toll-free) 1-800-237-5031
Fax: (902) 368-4236
e-mail: peihr@isn.net

www.gov.pe.ca/humanrights/

QUEBEC
Commission de droits de la personne et des droits de la jeunesse
360 Saint-Jacques Street, 2nd floor
Montreal, PQ H2Y 1P5
Tel.: (toll-free) 1-800-361-6477
TTY: (514) 873-2648
Fax: (514) 873-6032

www.cdpdj.qc.ca

SASKATCHEWAN
The Saskatchewan Human Rights Commission has an office in both Saskatoon and Regina.

Saskatchewan Human Rights Commission
Sturdy Stone Building
8th Floor, 122 3rd Avenue North
Saskatoon, SK S7K 2H6
Tel.: (toll-free) 1-800-667-9249
Fax: (306) 933-7863
e-mail: shrc@shrc.gov.sk.ca

Saskatchewan Human Rights Commission
1942 Hamilton Street, Suite 301
Regina, SK S4P 2C5
Tel.: (toll-free) 1-800-667-8577
Fax: (306) 787-0454
e-mail: shrc@shrc.gov.sk.ca

www.shrc.gov.sk.ca

YUKON
Yukon Human Rights Commission
201 211 Hawkins St.
Whitehorse, YT Y1A 1X3
Tel.: (toll-free) 1-800-661-0535
Fax: (867) 667-2662
e-mail: humanrights@yhrc.yk.ca

www.yhrc.yk.ca/

APPENDIX E
PRIVACY COMMISSIONERS IN CANADA

There are two reasons you might want to contact a privacy commissioner. One reason would be to make a complaint in connection with a violation of your privacy rights, such as a third party disclosure. You might also contact a privacy commissioner if a collection agency were not acting appropriately in response to your request for personal information in the collection agency's possession.

If you have been the victim of a third party disclosure by a collection agency, you can make a complaint to two different government regulators, the licensing administrator responsible for regulating collection agencies in your province and the government agency responsible for administering privacy laws in your province or territory. Appendix D, "Collection Agency Licensing Administrators," contains contact information for all the licensing administrators across Canada. This Appendix contains contact information for all the government agencies responsible for administering privacy laws in a particular province.

ALBERTA RESIDENTS
Alberta residents wishing to make a privacy-related complaint against a collection agency may want to file a complaint under the Alberta Personal Information Protection Act (PIPA). The complaint should be made to the Office of the Information and Privacy Commissioner of Alberta. The website for this office is http://www.oipc.ab.ca/.

BRITISH COLUMBIA RESIDENTS
If you are a British Columbia resident who wishes to make a privacy-related complaint, you can do so under the British Columbia Personal

Information Privacy Act (PIPA). Your complaint should be made to the Privacy Commissioner for British Columbia. The website for this office is www.oipc.bc.ca/.

QUEBEC RESIDENTS
A Quebec resident wanting to make a privacy-related complaint can do so under Quebec's Act Respecting the Protection of Personal Information in the Private Sector. The complaint should be made to the Commission d'accès à l'information du Québec. The website for this office is http://www.cai.gouv.qc.ca/.

PRIVACY COMPLAINTS UNDER PIPEDA
If you want to make a privacy-related complaint under the Personal Information Protection and Electronic Documents Act (PIPEDA), you can make your complaint to the Office of the Privacy Commissioner of Canada. You can learn more about this office by visiting its website at www.priv.gc.ca. You can obtain information about lodging a complaint by calling the Office of the Privacy Commissioner's Investigations Branch at 1-800-282-1376.

GLOSSARY

bankruptcy In exchange for surrendering certain property to a bankruptcy trustee, some, but perhaps not all, of a bankrupt's unsecured debts are forgiven.

bankruptcy trustee A person licensed under federal law to administer personal bankruptcies and consumer proposals.

bill collector An individual or an organization that collects money from consumers, including creditors, collection agencies, lawyers, or their employees.

Certificate of Discharge The document a person receives on the date his bankruptcy is finalized.

collateral An asset that can be seized by a creditor if a debtor fails to pay a debt. For example, when a consumer leases or purchases an automobile on credit, the car is the collateral.

collection agency A company that collects money from consumers on behalf of others and obtains at least half of its revenues from doing so. This includes traditional collection agencies as well as law firms engaged in high-volume debt collection work.

collector A person who collects debts.

consolidation loan A loan that a person uses to pay off his existing debts.

consumer debt A debt incurred by a person for goods, services, or a loan. Consumer debt does not include money owing to the government or money owing for child or spousal support.

consumer proposal A formal arrangement made through a bankruptcy trustee under which a person repays a percentage of his unsecured debts over a period of up to five years.

credit counselling agency An organization that arranges the repayment of *all* of a person's unsecured debts, over a period of up to five years.

creditor A company to which a person owes a debt. The original creditor is the firm that provided a person with goods, services, a loan, or some form of credit. A creditor can also be a company that has purchased a debt.

credit rating A number (R0, R1, R2, R3, R4, R5, R7, or R9) on a person's credit report that shows how current he is with his bill payments on a specific account.

credit reporting agency A for-profit company that gathers information on consumers' creditworthiness and makes it available where permitted by law.

credit score A number between 300 and 900 that credit reporting agencies use to rate a person's creditworthiness. A credit reporting agency will take into consideration several factors when determining a person's credit score, including repayment history.

Criminal Code A federal law protecting the public from numerous offences. The contravention of any of these laws constitutes criminal behaviour.

damages Financial compensation awarded by a court to a successful plaintiff in a lawsuit.

date of discharge The date when a bankrupt receives his Certificate of Discharge from bankruptcy and is released from liability for certain debts.

date of insolvency The date when a person files for personal bankruptcy.

debt buyer or **debt purchaser** A company other than the consumer's original creditor that owns a specific debt.

debt management plan A plan arranged by a credit counselling agency on behalf of an individual under which he repays 100 per cent of the money he owes to certain creditors over a period of up to five years.

debtor A person, partnership, or corporation that owes money to a creditor. In this book a debtor is sometimes referred to as a consumer – or simply "you."

debt settlement The process whereby a person settles one or more debts for less than 100 cents on the dollar.

default judgment A judgment awarded by the courts when a person fails to file an appropriate defence in a timely fashion.

defence The document a defendant files with the appropriate court in response to a lawsuit that has been initiated against him.

dialer An expensive piece of hardware used by bill collectors to dial thousands of telephone numbers in a relatively short period of time.

discharged bankrupt A person who has received his Certificate of Discharge from bankruptcy and is no longer liable for certain debts. Until then, he is referred to as an undischarged bankrupt.

double A collector has a person speak to a second collector during the course of a single call, to reinforce the importance of paying an outstanding account or meeting a payment deadline.

enforcement remedies The options available to a creditor that has received a judgment against a person that help it collect the debt, such as wage garnishments.

exemption from wage garnishment The portion of a person's wages that are exempt from a wage garnishment in a specific province or territory.

exempt property Property belonging to a person that by law cannot be seized by a bankruptcy trustee or judgment creditors.

first assigns When a person's delinquent account has been placed with its first collection agency for collection.

for-profit credit counselling agency A credit counselling agency run for profit. For-profit credit counselling agencies typically charge their clients a fee of 15 per cent of the dollar amount of debts included in a debt management plan.

garnishment When a court orders someone owing money to a debtor (such as an employer or a bank) to pay certain money into court for distribution to one or more creditors.

insolvent A person is considered insolvent when (1) the dollar value of his debts is greater than the dollar value of his assets, and (2) he is unable to meet his financial obligations as they become due.

judgment A court order stating that a debtor owes a specific sum of money to a specific creditor.

judgment creditor A creditor that has obtained a judgment against a debtor.

judgment debtor A debtor whose creditor has obtained a judgment against him.

judgment proof A debtor is immune from having a judgment against him enforced because he has no assets or sources of income available.

limitation periods The period of time in which a creditor must sue a person on a debt. The limitation periods for simple contract debt are two years in Alberta, Ontario, and Saskatchewan; three years in Quebec; and six years in the rest of Canada.

lump sum payment A single payment of money. In most instances when a debt is settled, it is done with a lump sum payment.

Master Credit Agreement A contract under which a financial institution agrees to make a certain amount of credit available to a person in exchange for collateral (usually a mortgage).

non-exempt property A person's property that can potentially be seized by judgment creditors and that must be surrendered to a bankruptcy trustee when a person files for bankruptcy.

non-profit credit counselling agency A credit counselling agency that is not run for profit.

original creditor The creditor that provided a person with goods, services, a loan, or some form of credit.

payment in full When 100 per cent of the debt owing is paid. In contrast, under a settlement in full, a creditor accepts a payment of less than 100 per cent of the amount owing in order to resolve a debt.

Personal Information Protection and Electronic Documents Act (PIPEDA) A federal privacy law that protects individuals' right to privacy. It also gives individuals the right to obtain personal information that organizations have on file about them.

personal property Any property other than land.

pre-approved settlement instructions Rules a creditor provides to its collection agent for settling accounts.

privacy commissioner A senior civil servant responsible for administering a privacy law.

prohibited collection practices Behaviour on the part of collection agencies and their employees that is prohibited under provincial and territorial law.

proof of payment Proof that a person made a payment on his account.

purchased debt Debt owned by someone other than the original creditor.

real property Also known as "real estate," it includes a house, townhouse, condominium, cottage, farm, or rental property.

receipt A written acknowledgment that a payment of a specific dollar amount has been made.

release letter A letter from a collection agency stating that a specific account has been resolved and no additional money is owing.

second assigns The name given to a delinquent account after it is recalled from the first collection agency it was assigned to and subsequently placed with a second collection agency.

secured debt A debt for which a creditor has some collateral or security that it can turn to if the borrower doesn't pay. For example, when a person borrows money to purchase or lease an automobile, the lender will typically put a lien on the automobile.

settlement in full When a creditor accepts one or more payments totalling less than 100 per cent of the balance owing, in order to resolve an account.

settlement letter A letter, typically prepared by a collection agency, that outlines the terms under which a creditor is prepared to accept one or more payments as settlement in full.

"Silverthorn Lite" debt settlement strategy A strategy a person can use to try and eliminate one or more unsecured consumer debts for approximately 20 to 35 cents on the dollar, and sometimes less. Under this strategy the person stops making payments to certain unsecured creditors, and after an outstanding account has been in default for 24 to 36 months, he negotiates lump sum settlements with his creditors.

"Silverthorn Max" debt settlement strategy A variation of the "Silverthorn Lite" debt settlement strategy. A person waits for the limitation period to expire on his debts, and then either (1) doesn't pay the account, or (2) negotiates a settlement.

small claims court A court in which civil lawsuits below a certain dollar amount are heard. In small claims court it is very common for the parties to represent themselves, or they may be represented by a paralegal or a lawyer.

statute of limitations The provincial or territorial law that outlines limitation periods for different categories of lawsuits.

Superintendent of Bankruptcy The federal official responsible for administering the Bankruptcy and Insolvency Act.

surplus income payments The payments that a person filing for personal bankruptcy must make to his bankruptcy trustee when he has an income above a certain threshold. This obligation ends when he obtains his Certificate of Discharge from bankruptcy.

Sheriff An officer responsible for executing a writ or some other process of the court. In some instances the duties of a Sheriff will be carried out by a bailiff.

Statement of Affairs A document completed by a person filing for personal bankruptcy that lists all of his unsecured debts.

statute A law passed by the Parliament of Canada or a provincial legislature.

third assigns Outstanding accounts placed with a collection agency for the third time. Delinquent accounts will often be referred to as third assigns even when they have already been assigned three or more times.

third party disclosure The disclosure of personal information to someone who is not entitled by law to receive this information. In the context of debt collection, a third party disclosure occurs when a bill collector discloses the existence or details of a debt to anyone other than (1) the debtor, (2) the debtor's representative, (3) an individual the debtor has authorized to discuss the debt with the creditor, (4) the bill collector's lawyer or authorized collection agent, or (5) another person legally responsible for the debt.

undischarged bankrupt A person who has filed for personal bankruptcy and has not yet obtained his discharge from bankruptcy.

unsecured debt A debt where the creditor has no collateral or security in the event of the debtor's non-payment.

wage garnishment A court order under which a creditor seeks to seize a portion of a person's wages from his employer.

writ of execution A court order authorizing a sheriff or court officer to seize property belonging to a debtor.

ACKNOWLEDGMENTS

To three individuals who spent many hours sharing their insights with me, bankruptcy trustees Doug Hoyes and Ted Michalos, with the firm of Hoyes Michalos & Associates, as well as Margaret Johnson, President of Solutions Credit Counselling Service Inc., who has a wealth of experience in collections and credit counselling.

To numerous individuals with extensive backgrounds in the collection industry, whose identities must remain anonymous, who read the manuscript and critiqued it.

To my agent, Arnold Gosewich, who encouraged me to write this book.

To the publishers at McClelland & Stewart for their enthusiastic support of this project.

To my editor, Trena White, with whom it was a pleasure to work preparing the manuscript.

To designer Terri Nimmo for designing the book cover and contributing a number of visual enhancements.

To Jarret Austin and Paul Stewart of Nautalex Business Services Inc., who believed in this book from the beginning.

To my daughters, Teresa and Veronica, who missed more than a few weekend afternoons with their father because of this book.

And most of all to my parents, Frank and Shirley, without whom this book would not have been possible.

INDEX

family and friends: abused by collector, 224, 259; acting as guarantor for, 96; answering calls for you, 47; and collector tactics, 45–46, *50;* as guarantor, 144; and joint bank accounts, *84,* 94; owing money to, 144; transferring assets to, fraudulence of, 96–97
farmers, 87
financial hardship: as factor in settlement, 119–21, 133–34; makes judgment enforcement difficult, 91
financial institutions. *See* banks
fines: by court, 193; by government, 10
first assign, 14, 132
fishers, 87
fourth assign, 14, 132
fraud, by you, *28,* 96–97, 193

garnishments: from bank accounts, 84; false threats of, 229–30; how they work, 80–81; laws against, in New Brunswick, 22, 80–81, *82,* 83; and people with low-paying jobs, 77–78, 81–83, 87; protecting wages from, 70, 81–83, 88–90, *181;* types, 80; of wages, 81–83, 88–89, 165, 171
government: and limitation periods on debts, 61, 65; options for resolving debt, *102, 108,* 144, 152, 203; poor regulation of collection agencies, 219; powers to collect debts, 11–12, 71, 85; types of debts, 8, 10–11
GST, 11, 71, 85

harassment: collection calls, 246–48; criminal, 249
health, as factor in settlement, 133
homes: as collateral for secured debts, 9; mortgages, 9, 106, 149; risk of seizure or lien, 85–88, 95, 184, 190, 194–95, 229
Home Trust, 129
human rights: making complaints

about, 224–26, 259–60; provincial and territorial tribunals, 275–81; violations by collectors, 224

identity theft, *28*
impersonating a police officer, 250–51
income: and bankruptcy, 190–91; creditor's ability to identify, 86; and likelihood of lawsuit, 74, 77–78; and wage garnishment, 77–78, 81–83
income taxes: as government debt, 10; payable on RRSP withdrawals, 107; refunds clawed back if money owed to government, 71, 85
inheritance: garnishment of, 80; used to pay debt, 149
insolvency, 177–78, 180, *195,* 203
instalment payments: advantages and disadvantages, 107, 114–15, 200; aggressive payment strategy, 110–14; conservative payment strategy, 110; costs, 204; defined, 10, 103; for government debt, *108;* negotiated vs. unilateral, 107; and Silverthorn Max, 164; under consumer proposal, 182; using postdated cheques for, 107–8, 109
insurance, and credit rating, 100
interest on debt: and credit score, 25; finding out if frozen, *112;* and instalment payments, 111–12; and settlements, 122
interest relief, on Canada Student Loans, 13
Internet bills, 9, 118
Internet, social networking sites, 46

jail, 100, 250
joint bank accounts, *84,* 94
judgment creditor, defined, 79
judgment debtor, defined, 79
judgment proof, 86–88, 166
judgments: and burden of proof, 68–69; creditor's ability to enforce, 75, 79–86; creditor's lack of ability

personal information: getting your files from an agency, 239–45; keeping confidential, *73, 84,* 93, 150–51

Personal Information Protection and Electronic Documents Act (PIPEDA), 49, 241–45, 258–59, 283

personal property: and bankruptcy, 190; creditor's ability to identify, 86; defined, 10; false threats about, 229–30; risk of seizure, 85–86, 87–88

police officer, impersonating, 250–51

Prince Edward Island: collection agency licensing, 272; exemptions from wage garnishments, *83;* Human Rights Commission, 280; limitation period on debts, *63;* no right to stop calls from collection agencies, 36; times when collectors cannot call, *265*

privacy: getting your files from an agency, 239–45; illegal collector behaviours, 232; laws against disclosing your debt to anyone but you, 49–50, 222–24, 258–59; making complaints about, 258–59, 282; provincial, territorial, and federal laws and contacts, 241–42, 282–83

proof of debt: asking collector for, 53, 67–68; and debt buyers, 53, 137–38; laws regulating, 227–28; and lawsuits, 68–70

property. *See* personal property; real property

property taxes, 8–10

provinces and territories: collection agency or collector licensing and regulating, 219, 224, 235, 256–58, 267–74; collection calls, how to stop, 36–37, 39–40; and collection calls to someone other than the debtor, *53;* collection call times, 33, 35, 230, *265;* consumer protection from collectors, 16–17, 20, *22,* 35, 56, 226–32, *265;* creditor regulating,

255–56; credit reporting agency regulating, 25, 233–35; credit reports, duration of information, 30; and enforcement remedies available to creditors, 80–85; exemptions to property seizure, 87–88; exemptions to wage garnishments, 88, 91; human rights commissions and tribunals, 275–81; human rights protection, 224–25; privacy rights, 224; statutes of limitations on debt, 16, 61–62, *63–64,* 64–66, 199–200; student loans, 12–13

provincial taxes, 10–11

publicity, negative, for creditor, 78, 253, 260

Quebec: collection agency licensing, 272–73; exemptions from wage garnishments, *83;* how to stop collection calls in, 36–37, 40; human rights commission, 280; limitation period on debts, 61, *62,* 66, 178, 199–200; privacy commissioner contact information, 283; privacy rights, 241–42; protection of consumers from collectors, 227, 228, *265;* and Silverthorn Lite, 142, 153; and Silverthorn Max, 165; student loans, 12

race, abused by collector, 224, 259

real estate agents, 80, 83

real property: borrowing against, to avoid lawsuits, 95–96; creditor's ability to identify, 86; defined, 10; false threats about, 229–30; liens on, 84; and likelihood of lawsuit, 74; preventing seizure of, 90; risk of seizure, 85–86, 87–88

records, of communications, *13,* 55, 234, 236–38

religion, abused by collector, 224, 259

rental income, 12, 80

resources: collection agency regulating authorities, 267–74; debt identification worksheet, *264;* getting your